Affects, Cognition, and Language as Foundations of Human Development

Affects, Cognition, and Language as Foundations of Human Development considers human development from the three most basic systems—affects (our earliest feelings), cognition, and language. Holinger explores how these systems enhance potential and help prevent problems, both in individuals and in societies.

He begins with a focus on the affects of interest and anger and how affects provide the foundation for the sense of self and playing and creating. The author delves into cognition in the context of human relationships and infants' remarkable capacity to understand language long before they can talk. Drawing on the work of Darwin, Freud, Stern, Basch, and the ground-breaking ideas of Silvan Tomkins, this work thus deepens the exploration into human development by integrating affects, cognition, and language. The author also uses this triad to examine two important societal issues: physical punishment, bias, prejudice, and violence.

This book will not only appeal to psychologists, psychoanalysts, psychiatrists, and social workers but is also accessible to parents, educators, and policymakers.

Paul C. Holinger, MD, MPH, is a Psychiatrist, Training and Supervising Analyst, and Child and Adolescent Supervising Analyst. Dr. Holinger is a Faculty Member and former Dean at the Chicago Psychoanalytic Institute and retired Professor of Psychiatry at Rush University Medical Center, Chicago, Illinois.

"Paul C. Holinger offers the professional community and the general public a brilliant integration of humanitarian and scientific approaches to child development. His presentation of the interplay of affects, cognition, and language as foundational elements of human development reflects his extensive experience and deep respect for the uniqueness of each individual. The impact of societal problems—physical punishment, bias, prejudice, and violence—on child development is presented in terms that constitute a call to action for parents, educators, and mental health professionals; for anyone committed to protecting children's developmental potential."
    Harriet Wolfe, *MD, President, International Psychoanalytical Association*

"Paul Holinger's book is, above all else, a message of hope. In exploring the origins and factors of healthy human development and explaining them in certain, clear-eyed terms, Dr. Holinger operates on the belief that when we know better, we will do better. He clarifies the murky early years of parenting and reframes moments that can feel frustrating into observations of what is, truly, quite fascinating about tiny, growing humans. Our children and our society are counting on us to heed Dr. Holinger's call and lean into our full humanity so that every child gets a chance to reach their full, innate potential."
    Heidi Stevens, *Nationally Syndicated Columnist*

"Paul Holinger has written a must-read for parents, therapists, and legislators alike. If you've ever wondered why we do what we do or how to help someone or a society change, this is your go-to book. Using the concepts of affect, cognition, and language, he synthesizes an enormous body of research through clear anecdotes and case vignettes. As if that wasn't enough, he goes on to explain why, against all the evidence, we continue to use physical punishment as well as why we treat other types of people in such destructive, prejudicial ways."
    Daniel W. Prezant, *PhD, President of the American Psychoanalytic Association*

"In *Affects, Cognition, and Language as Foundations of Human Development*, Paul Holinger has produced a tour de force. In an elegant, engaging volume, he describes the intertwining of affects, cognition, and language in human development. In clear language, he unpacks the impact of these complex interactions on individual treatment, parenting, and crucial social issues such as violence. This volume can serve as a cross-disciplinary foundational text for many mental health programs."
    Leon Hoffman, *MD, Center for Regulation Focused Psychotherapy*

"In this book, Paul Holinger effectively integrates knowledge about the 'information systems' of affects, cognition, and language to create a new lens for looking at normal and pathological development through the life cycle. Clinicians, teachers, parents, and policymakers can fruitfully apply this illuminating perspective to address children's needs in multiple contexts, ranging from child rearing to therapy to crucial social issues, as Holinger illustrates in his cogent discussion of physical violence and punishment. The reader comes away inspired with hope by Holinger's clarity and commitment to the needs of children and all who care for them."

Jack Novick, *PhD, and* **Kerry Kelly Novick**, *Psychoanalysts and Authors of* Working With Parents Makes Therapy Work *and* Freedom to Choose: Two Systems of Self-Regulation

"Paul C. Holinger, MD, MPH, has written a canonical text in *Affect, Cognition, and Language as Foundations for Human Development*. He takes the reader on an exciting journey through the intricate interplay of these 'messy' information processing systems. He shows how infants and children thrive where interest and curiosity have been encouraged. All this is done while tracing out the history of human development, including cutting-edge research and illuminating case studies. The author does not shy away from tackling the most pressing issues facing societies—prejudice, bias, racism, hatred, and violence. This is a gem of a book offering a roadmap as to what needs to be done for a healthy society. He not only leaves us with the challenge to take up the task to do better; he inspires us to do so as well. The book is a gift to humanity."

Nancy Hartevelt Kobrin, *PhD, Psychoanalyst; Counter Terrorist Expert; and Author of* The Jihadi Dictionary: The Essential Intel Tool for Military, Law Enforcement, Government and the Concerned Public

"In this remarkable book, Paul Holinger creatively continues the thinking on affects that Darwin introduced in 1872. Darwin's work almost got lost in psychology until the work of Silvan Tomkins in the middle of the twentieth century. Since then, a number of scholars have extended the thinking about affects into the meaning of language, development, and the self. Holinger intelligently integrates these diverse strands into a cohesive whole. He further suggests the relevance of his model for understanding topics as wide-ranging as cults, racist extremism, and cognitive functioning. I warmly recommend this book for its fresh approach to subjects often slighted in psychological, social, and historical scholarship."

Charles B. Strozier, *PhD, Professor of History at John Jay College; Psychoanalyst; and Author of* Heinz Kohut: The Making of a Psychoanalyst, Lincoln's Quest for Union, *and* The New World of the Self

"Paul Holinger, our experienced guide, takes us on a journey into the developing mind, tracing the trajectory from early affects to cognition and then language, each phase enriching the other. In jargon-free and often quite personal writing, we learn how affects are the foundation of being human and how they blossom under the caring spirit of the attuned caregiver. Holinger demonstrates how empathy is the medium that allows for the enlivening link between affects and words. Clear clinical examples animate these concepts, along with demonstrations of attuned interventions. He shares with us in some detail a passion that he has devoted himself to throughout his career. That is, an understanding of the levels of damage that physical punishment inflicts on the growing mind and spirit. This is not to be missed. This and his understanding of the corrosive impact of malignant 'othering' make the book a worthy read. So does the sparkling 'gleam in his eye' that he describes in caretakers that we readers also can feel in his graceful writing."
Harvey Schwartz, *MD, Producer and Host, IPA Podcast*, Psychoanalysis On and Off the Couch

"A remarkable tour de force . . . With deep scientific knowledge and support, but written to be readily accessible to all, Dr. Holinger's manuscript should be read by all, and especially by new parents. The insights about infants and children that are provided form an invaluable foundation for raising curious, empathic, emotionally healthy, and downright delightful children."
Daniel L. Goldberg, *JD, Boston, Massachusetts*

"Dr. Holinger's fascinating and ground-breaking book explores the origins of our earliest feelings (affects), thinking, and language—thus paving the way for a better understanding of human nature and development. In addition to discussing individuals and clinical cases, he also sheds new light on two major societal problems: physical punishment; and bias, prejudice, and violence. This is an essential book for mental health professionals, educators, and parents, and it is a must-read in our troubled times."
Pamela C. Cantor, *PhD, Author of* Understanding Children and Youth

"Dr. Holinger provides a masterful integration of three core developmental domains, powerfully demonstrating the complexity and beauty of children's experience of the world. This work is all the evidence we need to end the shame and humiliation of physical punishment, which offends the miraculous unfolding of the mind."
Joan Durrant, *PhD, Executive Director, Positive Discipline in Everyday Life; Professor (Senior Scholar), Department of Community Health Sciences, Max Rady College of Medicine, Rady Faculty of Health Sciences; and Author of* Positive Discipline in Everyday Parenting

"*Affects, Cognition, and Language as Foundations of Human Development*, Paul Holinger's newest book, arrives just in time. Dr. Holinger builds on the three core foundations in Part 1, where together we explore two critical societal problems: the physical punishment of children and the origins and persistence of bias, prejudice, and violence. For workplaces virtually paralyzed by hypersensitivities, extreme polarities, and threats of violence, Paul's insights provide hope. Hope, that with understanding, we can pull on the right threads to undo these two self-made Gordian knots."

David E. "Daven" Morrison III, *MD, Clinical Associate Professor of Psychiatry and Behavioral Sciences, Chicago Medical School; Academy of Organizational and Occupational Psychiatry—Past President; Group for the Advancement of Psychiatry (GAP); Committee on Work and Psychiatry; and Author of* The A.B.C.'s of Behavioral Forensics

"In times such as these, there seems nothing more important than to understand what makes human beings tick and to use that knowledge to live more deeply human and humane lives. If Silvan Tomkins, the grandfather of the modern-day study of emotion, was correct in following Darwin's lead by declaring our affect system as the primary motivational system in human beings, then we surely need to better understand affect and emotion across human development. I believe that Tomkins was 100 percent correct, and I also believe that Paul Holinger's new book is a superb elucidation of what we need to understand about affect, cognition, and language. This book will be illuminating and extremely helpful to parents and professionals alike."

Lauren Abramson, *PhD, Founding Director, Community Transformation (www.communitytransformation.net), and Restorative Justice Facilitator, Trainer, Writer, and Theorist*

"This provocative book describes a bold thesis that links infants' subcortical reactions to several contemporary social problems. Key foundational scholars who led Holinger to home in on the developmental processes integrating affect, cognition, and language in thought-provoking juxtapositions are identified. Vignettes nicely illustrate Holinger's points, and clinical implications are provided to make this book appealing to a wide range of readers, including parents, educators, therapists, and scientists."

George W. Holden, *PhD, Emeritus Professor, SMU President of the US Alliance to End the Hitting of Children*

"Paul Holinger conveys the wisdom of a lifetime as he synthesizes the latest research in child development and brings this to life with clinical examples, personal anecdotes, and quotes from thinkers from Aristotle to Martin Luther King. While the book's title might seem daunting, it will prove enlightening and an enjoyable read for parents, clinicians, educators, policy makers, and pretty much anyone curious about how affect, cognition, and language apply to parenting, psychotherapy, and social policy."

Arthur Nielsen, *MD, Clinical Professor of Psychiatry and Behavioral Sciences, Feinberg School of Medicine, Northwestern University; Faculty, Chicago Psychoanalytic Institute;* and *Author of* A Roadmap for Couple Therapy *and* Integrative Couple Therapy in Action

Affects, Cognition, and Language as Foundations of Human Development

Paul C. Holinger

Routledge
Taylor & Francis Group
LONDON AND NEW YORK

Designed cover image: Composite of Getty Images by Sensvector, Hope and Melita

First published 2025
by Routledge
4 Park Square, Milton Park, Abingdon, Oxon OX14 4RN

and by Routledge
605 Third Avenue, New York, NY 10158

Routledge is an imprint of the Taylor & Francis Group, an informa business

© 2025 Paul C. Holinger

The right of Paul C. Holinger to be identified as author of this work has been asserted in accordance with sections 77 and 78 of the Copyright, Designs and Patents Act 1988.

All rights reserved. No part of this book may be reprinted or reproduced or utilised in any form or by any electronic, mechanical, or other means, now known or hereafter invented, including photocopying and recording, or in any information storage or retrieval system, without permission in writing from the publishers.

Trademark notice: Product or corporate names may be trademarks or registered trademarks, and are used only for identification and explanation without intent to infringe.

British Library Cataloguing-in-Publication Data
A catalogue record for this book is available from the British Library

ISBN: 978-0-367-19634-9 (hbk)
ISBN: 978-0-367-19635-6 (pbk)
ISBN: 978-0-429-20364-0 (ebk)

DOI: 10.4324/9780429203640

Typeset in Times New Roman
by Apex CoVantage, LLC

For Joni and Campbell

Contents

Foreword		*xiii*
CLAUDIA LAMENT		
Preface		*xvi*
Acknowledgments		*xvii*

PART 1
Developing   1

1. Developing: Exploring Human Development via Affects, Cognition, and Language   3
2. The Evolving Concept of Affects   10
3. Current Concepts of Affects: Functions and Examples   19
4. The Affect of Interest: The Core of Our Existence   34
5. Affects: The Foundation of Playing and Creating   46
6. Affects, Early Development, and the Sense of Self   54
7. Anger: The Misunderstood Affect   63
8. Emerging Cognition   72
9. Language: Before Children Begin to Talk   81
10. Affects Into Words: When Children Begin to Talk   87
11. Integrating Affects, Cognition, and Language: The Impact of Early Verbalization of Affects, the Emergence of Empathy, and Clinical Implications   95

PART 2
**Societal Implications of Understanding Affects,
Cognition, and Language: Views on Overcoming
Physical Punishment and Bias, Prejudice, and Violence** 111

    Introduction to Part 2: Physical Punishment and Toward
    Understanding Bias, Prejudice, and Violence 113

12 Physical Punishment: "The Canary in the Coal Mine" 116

13 Toward Understanding Bias, Prejudice, and Violence 133

14 Wrapping Up and a Glance at the Future 148

    References *150*
    Index *161*

Foreword

When reading Paul C. Holinger, one comes away wondering whether one has read a humanist's perspective on the world or a scientist's? These twin identities that abide cheek by jowl within his work are revealed in his deep respect for the integrity, unique qualities, and innate worth of each individual. His care in thinking about the provision of the nutrients that will release children's potential to open themselves to the discovery of who they are never falters. This devotion to humanism is equally matched by his steadfast dedication to science and its evolution through the ages. His writing breathes with the air that encircles both domains.

For parents, educators, and baby watchers, in general, understanding how infants and young children express their feelings can be a mysterious, if not daunting, enterprise. In one of his previous books, *What Babies Say Before They Can Talk: The Nine Signals Infants Use to Express Their Feelings* (Holinger, 2003), Holinger drew back the curtain on this world to illuminate the fact that very often, a child's behaviors do not accurately capture the emotions that lie beneath them.

In this new volume, Holinger expands upon this truth and takes the reader on a fascinating journey through three principal elements that undergird psychological development: affects, cognition, and language. It is in probing their *interactivity*, their mutual influences upon each other, that Holinger makes a fresh contribution to the understanding of how children develop.

Having wisely decided to use descriptive and vivid language unfettered by professional jargon to make his case, he integrates the domains of biology, neurobiology, developmental psychology, and psychoanalysis to help us see the nature of the interrelatedness of these three foundational functions of the mind. With examples culled from patients, friends, family members, and even memories of and reveries about his own childhood, Holinger underscores the importance of how the coordination of affect, cognition, and language supplies an organic counterbalance to each while releasing their unified potential to facilitate children's growth. In so doing, interest, curiosity, and wonderment seize the day. Indeed, if Holinger prizes one feature of human life over any others, I believe that he would land on his reverence for children's ability to transform affects into creative forms that reflect those distinctive qualities that make each of them who they are.

Holinger shows how play naturally fosters creativity whereby the triad of affect, cognition, and language—including even, before the utterance of the word, the preverbal—participate in a dance of transformation. Here is where the imagination takes the child or the adult to a new land of possibility where a never-before-imagined self can come to life.

Of particular importance to parents, caregivers, and therapists, Holinger's reflections also bring the reader's attention to those *obstacles* that constrain children's freshness of spirit—that necessary, unbridled, carefree domain to delight in make-believe and play with dreams of who they might become. While he foregoes easy answers about how to connect with and foster the unique qualities of each child's interior house, peopled as it might be with dragons and demons and witches and gods, he also demonstrates how falling short of doing so may lead to the inhibition of creativity.

With compassion and sensitivity to the adult who tends to children, he illuminates how understandable misunderstandings can develop between a caregiver's attempts to decode children's feelings and the, at times, baffling and indirect ways with which they may convey them. For instance, if the adult fails to intuit the vulnerability and fear that is hidden behind tantrums and outbursts, the caregiver may punish or shame the child, thereby eliciting fear and anger, such that over time the child internalizes the aggressive qualities of the shaming adult and berates themselves.

While cognition is the seat of thinking, reasoning, judgment, self-reflection, perception, and reality testing, Holinger brings his own creative thinking to how cognitive capabilities ripen over the earliest years of a child's life. Here is where he astutely brings in one of the most significant functions of language: its ability to bring words to the world of thought. Language buttresses cognition and affect, as it promotes a child's ability to communicate inner thoughts and feelings both to self and the outside world. Through Holinger's keen eye, the reader can visualize how this triad's intrinsic synchronization can help or hinder the developmental process, enhance therapeutic activities and family relationships, and even reach into the realm of understanding the complex nature of the individual's relationship to the greater social polity.

To this latter point, the reader is shepherded into how the convergence of cognition, affect, and language shapes society for good and ill. The Czech poet Miroslav Holub—who was also an immunologist—envisioned the function of drama as akin to the immune system within the human body. What he meant was that the creative spirit is a staunch protector against oppressive forces within the prevailing culture that seeks to root out the individual's precious potential for self-discovery and crush it. Holinger's efforts as both humanist and scientist also foster immunity against society's aggression toward the burgeoning self.

Through his investigations, he discovered that in a group setting, fear and anger in excess can be likened to SOS signals. They telegraph to those who are listening and can decipher these signals that the group mind's rational thinking may be headed toward a meltdown. Such situations can lead to toxic, cruel behaviors that appear in weaponized, racist language and even devolve further into acts of physical brutality. In group-think, the language of misinformation that is believed to hold truths is hurled at the targeted other with the aim of instigating the masses toward violent actions. Holinger provides contemporary examples in Nazi propaganda, anti-vax theories during the COVID-19 pandemic, and QAnon conspiracy beliefs.

Fortunately, affect, cognition, and language can operate as a safeguard, or in Holinger's words, "a checks and balance feedback system" against such disturbing outcomes: putting feelings into words (mastering affect through spoken language) helps to temper confusing emotions. Through self-reflection, curiosity, and education about why a child misbehaves (engaging cognition) or why a group is frightened and enraged, impulsive actions may be delayed in favor of thoughtful contemplation.

Psychoanalysts, mental health professionals, scientists, parents, educators, and caregivers will find this book a wellspring of data about the remarkable fruits of the mutual influences of affect, cognition, and language that occur within the human mind. Culled from a rich source-base, Paul C. Holinger has succeeded in sounding a clarion call to the appreciation of the breathtaking potential of the developmental process—its joys but also its fragile nature. His work is to be read, read again, and cherished. He returns us to the foundations of the self and always, always restores the individual to the center of the conversation. We owe him a great debt of gratitude.

Claudia Lament[1]

Note

1 Claudia Lament, PhD; Former Editor-In-Chief, *The Psychoanalytic Study of the Child*.

Preface

It is wonderful to have worked for decades with children and adults, with so many remarkable teachers and colleagues, and to become aware of the many scholars and clinicians who have preceded me. This has fostered a tremendous sense of curiosity and given me an opportunity to consider human development from its origins—using what I call the triad of affects, cognition, and language.

My premise is that exploring development and clinical work from these perspectives can enhance individual potential and help prevent individual and social problems. In a sense, this work is a follow-up to *What Babies Say Before They Can Talk: The Nine Signals Infants Use to Express Their Feelings* (Holinger, 2003). That book dealt primarily with youngsters' feelings and has been translated into several languages. This current work deepens the exploration into human development, integrating affects, cognition, and language. I also use this triad to examine two important societal issues: physical punishment and bias, prejudice, and violence. Given the tremendous advances in understanding human development and clinical work, I have tried to make this book accessible to professionals in the psychological arena as well as to parents, educators, and policymakers. It seems incumbent to provide information and solutions to a larger audience and world.

To enhance the book, I have included several photographs. I was inspired to do this in part due to Sidney Blumenthal's ongoing, remarkable multivolume biography of Abraham Lincoln (beginning with *A Self-Made Man*, 2016), in which he included various pictures of people in Lincoln's saga, enlightening his narrative even further. Photographs convey a sense of visibility and credit to people, past and present, who have helped provide the world with a better understanding of human development.

Throughout this book, clinical and everyday narratives are used to illustrate various ideas and processes. The case examples in this book are disguised reconstructions from research experiences, supervisions, patients, and seminar discussions.

I hope you find this book as enlightening—and in many ways as entertaining—as I did in the process of writing it. We can only hope that our tomorrows, enhanced by a deeper appreciation of what makes us tick, will be filled with more curiosity, less fear, and more empathy for one another.

Paul C. Holinger, MD, MPH

Acknowledgments

I am profoundly grateful to the many people who have given so much of their time and knowledge to this project.

Let me begin by expressing my appreciation to those who read parts of this manuscript and shared their ideas over the years. So, thanks again to Lauren Abramson, Jim Anderson, Sue Baird, P. J. Barnett, Denia Barrett, Tom Barrett, Lynn Borenstein, Pam Cantor, Gary David, Joan Durrant, Stu Edelman, Kim Edelman, Rick Herrick, Campbell Holinger, Cecilia Holinger, Molly Holinger, Richard Holinger, William Holinger, Lynnae Holmes, Vick Kelly, Nancy Kobrin, Claudia Lament, Mary Lamia, Richard Lane, Ally Machate, Jeffrey McClough, Jill Mueller, Daven Morrison, Gavin Mullen, Art Nielsen, Jennifer Lock Oman, Regina Ryan, Joe Saginor, Neal Spira, Heidi K. Stevens, Chuck Strozier, David Terman, and Molly Witten.

I am extremely fortunate to have been involved with many people who were uniquely helpful in the development of this book through their teaching, guidance, logistical skills, and caregiving—thank you all so very much: C. Jama Adams, Virginia Barry, Michael Franz Basch, Helen Beiser, Tricia Berg, Barbara Berger, David Brooks, Willie Cade, Bert Cohler, the Chicago Psychoanalytic Institute Faculty, Students, and Staff, the Child/Adolescent Forum participants, Kirsten Dahl, Deborah DeLucia, Mary Doyle, Joan Dutton, William Dutton, Ron Ensom, Stephanie Farris, Robert Galatzer-Levy, Ben Garber, Kay Gallo, Paul Gallo, John Gedo, Elizabeth Gershoff, Jim Herzog, George Higgins, Leon Hoffman, Michael Hoit, George Holden, Dorothy Holinger, Jay Holinger, Lauren Holinger, Patsy Holinger, Clare Huntington, Charles Jaffe, Ramya Iyer, Ann Kaplan, Adele Kaufman, Ed Kaufman, Nikkie Kinziger, Elaine Klemen, Heinz Kohut, Marshall Kordon, Bonnie Litowitz, Norm Litowitz, Scott McCown, Jack Merriman, Ken Newman, Jack Novick, Kerry Kelly Novick, Susan Reed, Jennifer Rensner, Barrie Richmond, Barbara Rocah, Don Rosenblitt, George Russell, the St. Charles Public Library (IL), Erika Schmidt, Harvey Schwartz, Jorge Schneider, Henry Seidenberg, Alec Selwyn, Barbara Streeter, Phyllis Tyson, Trinity College (CT) Class of '68 group, Judy Yanof, Cindy Wiertel, Cliff Wilkerson, and Lizzie Zebro.

Pictures may be worth a thousand words, and perhaps especially when studying infants and development. I very much appreciate the opportunity to use photographs from the Cade, Orindo Holinger, and Kim families. In addition, many friends, family members, and colleagues have made some of the photographs throughout this book possible, including Gail Basch, Paul Gedo, and Tom Kohut.

To my patients, supervisees, and students, I owe a tremendous debt. Their collaborations with me in working with their goals and concerns have granted me immense learning and fulfillment.

My extreme gratitude to the following five collaborators to whom I am so indebted:

- Kalia Doner—for her organizing, wordsmithing, wisdom, humor, and so much more.
- Susannah Frearson—my editor at Routledge, for her oversight, ideas, and encouragement as the project progressed.
- Claudia Lament—for her integration of the concepts in this book and her vast knowledge of development and child/adolescent/adult psychoanalysis.
- Shelly Mabbs—for her remarkable work in procuring, preparing, and presenting the photographs.
- LeeAnn Pickrell—for her linguistic capacities, editing, and tracking over the last several months of the project.

And to Joni and Campbell, and to the pups Lanti TT and Sammy Small Paws (S^2P), you all have made this possible, and I cannot thank you enough.

Part 1

Developing

Chapter 1

Developing
Exploring Human Development via Affects, Cognition, and Language

Chapter Outline:
- Three information processing systems
- Affects, cognition, language: "Messy systems"
- Affects, cognition, and language as motivators of behaviors
- Other voices
- Defining development

I am fascinated by human development. For decades now, I have been fortunate to work with and study youngsters and adults, and this has fueled my focus on how we become who we are. And do we get a second chance? A third?

Why do I believe it is important to explore development? To enhance potential and prevent problems. Therefore, in this book, I want to examine human development and explore how we become the people we turn out to be.

Human development is remarkable in its inception and progressions. How might we try to understand development? Perhaps Abraham Lincoln's words from his "House Divided" speech (1858) might be useful:

> If we could first know where we are, and whither we are tending, we could better judge what to do, and how to do it.
>
> (White, 2005, p. 283)

This book has an overarching theme, namely, the importance and potential of our early years. Human beings are complex—but human development can be enhanced. As Heinz Kohut notes, "Childhood is a time when a properly empathic parental environment can mobilize the child's potential psychological strengths" (1994, p. 2). In a child, inborn human attributes interact with the external environment, creating opportunities and challenges, making it difficult to parse how personality evolves.

Daniel Stern's book *The Interpersonal World of the Infant* has been instrumental in understanding the early capacities of infants. For example, he states that "some senses of the self do exist long prior to self-awareness and language. These include the senses of agency, of physical cohesion, of continuity in time, of having intentions in mind, and other such experiences" (1985, p. 6). Recognizing infants' and children's emerging potentials highlights the significance of enhancing or impairing development.

Three Information Processing Systems

I focus on a crucial triad, what I call the three information processing systems in humans: *affects* (earliest feelings), *cognition*, and *language*. Many scholars and clinicians focus on one or two of these three issues, but that still leaves gaps in our understanding of development. When we consider these three elements together, development becomes much more understandable—both in individual human beings and in societies. As we explore these processes, we will see human beings use them to gain information that allows for adaptation and survival:

- *Affects* function as reactions to internal and external stimuli, contributing to our various motivations, behaviors, communication, and emotional development.
- *Cognition* includes thinking, memory, reality processing, perception (sight, smell, taste, hearing, touch, and others), self-reflection, learning, assessment of behaviors, and interpersonal skills.
- *Language* involves putting words and symbols to perceptions, ideas, and feelings, allowing for further communication with oneself and others.

It is difficult to overestimate the importance of such concepts in relation to development. Coordinating these systems permits us to enhance individual development and therapy, better understand family dynamics and outcomes, and improve social policies. They are the lenses through which we can explore the origins and problems of development. Infants and young children have remarkable capacities in these areas, and these attributes can be enhanced or derailed. It is vital to understand the power of affects, cognition, and language in shaping individuals and influencing social realities so that we can understand how the personal and societal converge.

I want to explore human development in a somewhat different way than usual. I have come to appreciate that development may usefully be characterized in part by the interactivity of these three innate information processing systems with each other and with the external environment over time. It is difficult for me to imagine understanding human development, clinical work with children and adults, and societal dynamics without explicitly taking affects, cognition, and language into account. The aim is to discuss these three systems, utilizing the contributions of people such as Donald Winnicott, Silvan Tomkins, Heinz Kohut, Daniel Stern, and many others, to create an increased understanding of these building blocks of personality and social structures.

First, regarding individual issues, I focus on the origins and functioning of affects, cognition, and language to the extent that current knowledge will allow and highlight how the integration of these processes has a powerful influence on an individual's development. These systems constitute a remarkable multifaceted arrangement, which, in the best of circumstances, provides an individual with checks-and-balances and, in the worst, creates problems of disorganization, dysfunction, and discord.

Second, I present ideas on how clinicians, educators, social policy professionals, and others might use these views to enhance potential and prevent problems on a societal level. Specifically, I explore how these aspects of development might impact understanding of issues such as physical punishment and bias, prejudice, and violence.

Affects, Cognition, Language: "Messy Systems"

So here's where it really gets interesting. All these information processing systems have profound liabilities as well as assets. They are what I call "messy systems." Each is a double-edged sword, with conscious and unconscious aspects.

For example, while affects can enhance emotional and intellectual growth, they may also be misunderstood, mislabeled, disorganizing, unconscious, or disavowed by us and others with whom we are interacting. We are prone to project and externalize our affects. For instance, we might deny our own anger, project it onto others, and see them as angry at us.

Cognition also has its problems. The thinking process involves both perception and response to that perception, conscious and unconscious. But what registers in the brain is not always a reflection of external consensual reality. We all have our own internal lenses through which we perceive the external world and ourselves, providing clarity and insight or clouding reality and creating confusion. The brain can be fooled by optical illusions, and we know that eyewitness accounts of a crime are notoriously unreliable. Faulty memory and false memory syndromes are also examples of compromised cognition and impaired reality processing.

Language, too, can create serious problems. Ideally, language functions as a tool for clear expression and perception. It can influence how a person internally shapes thoughts and feelings, and it can carry a person's internal reality out into the world to be shared with others. But, how adeptly a person uses language to convey internal realities accurately can vary widely within one person and from person to person. And misused or misshapen word choices can distort both internal perception and feelings and derail interactions with the environment.

Once language is involved, there is an opportunity for enhanced clarity or confusion. The same words can mean very different things to different people, resulting in misinterpretation and misunderstanding. As Daniel Stern stated eloquently,

> Language is a double-edged sword ... it drives a wedge between two simultaneous forms of interpersonal experience: as it is lived and as it is verbally represented.... Language, then causes a split in the experience of the self.
> (1985, pp. 162, 163)

Fortunately, language itself can be used to remedy misinterpretations. As linguist Bonnie Litowitz noted, "The use of language to talk about language allows us to discover if we are indeed 'getting the message,' are 'on the same page'" (2014, p. 302). But more on that in Chapters 9–11.

In short, in addition to the advantages of affects, cognition, and language, there are also liabilities that can create serious problems in the information processing systems of humans.

Affects, Cognition, and Language as Motivators of Behaviors

What about behaviors, you might ask? An interesting and important question. Affects, cognition, and language each contribute, to a greater or lesser extent, to motivating and shaping our behaviors—our actions or inactions, our responses to both internal and external stimulation.

As individuals and societies, we tend to focus on behaviors rather than the feelings and other issues that cause the behaviors. Consider, for example, the coverage of one of the frequent mass shootings in the United States. On May 24, 2022, at the Robb Elementary School in Uvalde, Texas, 21 people were killed. Unfortunately, coverage of incidents like this only touches on the surface issues and almost never gets to the root causes of such a tragedy. Law enforcement, the press, politicians, and policy officials often fail to explore the childhood psychopathology, the depression, the rage, the impulsivity, and the troubled home situations that may lead to the deadly action of an adolescent, teen, or adult.

We may ask, "Why were these issues not seen and their potential repercussions not understood and dealt with earlier—that is, possibly prevented—by the parents and other caregivers, the schools, friends, and society in general?" The answer is, in part: *Because as parents, teachers, and policymakers—we tend to focus on behaviors rather than the feelings that motivate the behaviors.*

At this point, allow me, please, to be a bit playful and personal (play is important throughout development, as we shall see). What follows are four "vignettes" that are examples of my efforts to understand development and the processes that underlie our behaviors.

The first involves an unusual publication from the early 20th century, as psychoanalysis was beginning to take hold. In 1925, August Aichhorn, a psychoanalyst in Vienna and colleague of Sigmund Freud, wrote a remarkable book called *Wayward Youth*. (Aichhorn, by the way, was one of Heinz Kohut's analysts). Aichhorn was a pioneer in that he studied, treated, and wrote about delinquent adolescents, showing how their feelings and backgrounds were contributing to their behaviors. This book was written for parents, teachers, and the public, in addition to professionals, and even today could be considered a must-read for these groups.

One hundred years later, it is still important to advocate for further exploration of the underlying processes of human development. Then, we have a better chance of utilizing these advances to understand individual and societal development.

The second example involves Daniel Stern's groundbreaking book *The Interpersonal World of the Infant* (1985). Daniel Stern was an important infant researcher

Photo 1.1 Daniel N. Stern
Source: Courtesy of the Stern Family

and psychoanalyst. Tucked away in the short Preface to his 1985 book is a poignant vignette about himself that highlights the importance and difficulty of understanding early development—infants and young children are not the same as adults! It is often very difficult for adults to understand infants and young children.

> When I was seven or so, I remember watching an adult try to deal with an infant of one or two years. At that moment it seemed to me so obvious what the infant was all about, but the adult seemed not to understand it at all . . . As an infant, I spent considerable time in the hospital, and in order to know what was going on, I became a watcher, a reader of the nonverbal. I never did grow out of it.
>
> (1985, p. ix)

These experiences may have contributed to motivating Stern's life work, thus helping us to understand early development better. In addition, you will see several examples of how understanding infants and young children and aspects of their development will help to elucidate their behaviors.

The third example is brief and involves my own early years. I am one of four children, all of us boys. As a youngster, I had experiences that puzzled me greatly. It seemed that there was a focus on behaviors—upsets, misbehaviors, and so on. Words were put to the behaviors, but not to the earlier issues and feelings that motivated the behaviors. And yet, in retrospect, it seems obvious that it was the feelings that were most crucial and causing the behaviors. However, I was certainly not able to articulate the dilemma as a child.

The last example is also a personal vignette. In my adolescence and early adulthood, I became increasingly interested in psychology and medicine, and I started doing some work and writing with my father. My father was a broncho-esophagologist, a surgeon specializing in the air (bronchi) and food (esophagus) passages. He used to say if you understood the beginnings of these structures—their embryology and origins—you could better understand how they develop, what could go wrong from inborn or external sources, and how to fix the problems. This seemed to be an interesting and important way to conceptualize these processes.

As I turned increasingly toward the psychological arena, the same ideas appeared useful with respect to an individual's personality as well as societal problems. In other words, what are the affects, cognition, and language issues that underlie and motivate behavior and character structure?

Is it complicated sometimes? Yes . . . but it's worth our efforts.

Other Voices

Many clinicians and scholars have contributed various conceptualizations to our understanding of human development. Some have addressed the very basics of development.

- Virginia Demos started at ground level when she proposed two basic human preferences: "coherence and organization" and "being an active agent in effecting the desired course of both internal and external events" (2019, p. 33).
- Similarly, Michael Basch stressed competence theory, which is striving for order, competence, and self-esteem (1988). Others have concentrated on specific developmental periods, such as infancy, adolescence, and so on.

I will discuss many of these contributors throughout this volume; however, a complete review is beyond my scope here. In addition, although my primary focus is on the psychological and psychoanalytic aspects of development, the advances in neurobiology are significant, and I will look at how they illuminate the psychological points of view (e.g., Panksepp, 1998; Gedo, 2005; Lane & Nadel, 2020).

Interestingly, over the years, the concepts of development themselves have shifted. Clearly defined chronological stages in linear models of development seem to have dominated initially (e.g., Erikson, Piaget). With the expansion to object-relations, relational psychology, two-person models, and greater emphasis on very early development, the focus on the importance of interaction with the environment has increased.

Over time, there has also been increasing interest in nonlinear models (e.g., S. Freud, 1915; Sander, 1962; A. Freud, 1965; Bowlby, 1969; Tyson, 2009; Galatzer-Levy, 2017; Demos, 2019; Lament, unpublished). The nonlinear perspective includes considering many variables, e.g., the innate information processing systems, genetics, environmental influences, and so on. Such models "predict that desirable development may follow many unpredictable routes to satisfactory and often similar outcomes ... Experiences will shape resulting development, but how they influence its development is not predictable" (Galatzer-Levy, 2017, pp. 82, 84). These experiences are innumerable and may be positive or negative: They can involve trauma, loss, an unusual opportunity, a specific physical or psychological talent or handicap, a relationship, psychotherapy, and so on.

Defining Development

With so many significant points of view, how do we begin to define development? For the purposes of this book, development is seen as what happens when the innate systems and the strengths and weaknesses of the individual interact with the opportunities and challenges of the environment. The goal is to explore how understanding the nature of affects, cognition, and language and their interactions with the environment throughout life may help us better appreciate how humans develop.

This book is divided into two sections. The first section deals with affects (Chapters 2–7), cognition (Chapter 8), language (Chapters 9–10), and integration of these three systems (Chapter 11). The second section considers social policy and the impact of these three processes on two major societal concerns: physical punishment (Chapter 12) and bias, prejudice, and violence (Chapter 13). The book concludes with a brief wrap-up (Chapter 14).

Chapter 2

The Evolving Concept of Affects

Chapter Outline

- The evolution of the concept of affects
- What are the various affects?
- Summarizing

There are a variety of disciplines and conceptual models that strive to provide an understanding of affects, which raises important questions.

- Are affects innate responses that evolve into emotions and feelings as a newborn, growing child, adolescent, and adult interact with their external environment? Or are they full-blown feelings and emotions from their first manifestation?
- Are the affects of interest, enjoyment, surprise, distress, anger, fear, shame, disgust, and dissmell (aversion to an odor) words that accurately describe a person's responses to subjective experiences? Or are they describing behavioral manifestations of internal responses to stimuli? Or both?
- Are affects conscious or unconscious, or both?
- How are they related to drives? Are they shaped by them? Can they modify drives?

This book leans on the work of Charles Darwin, Silvan Tomkins, Michael Basch, Donald Nathanson, and others to clarify the nature of affects. Therefore, following a brief discussion of Darwin and Freud, the focus will be on the work of Tomkins, his colleagues, and other psychologists, psychoanalysts, neurobiologists, and developmentalists involved in this work. The aim is to discuss and differentiate affects from emotions, feelings, and drives.

The following quotes give a good overview of the evolving definitions of affects over the past 70 years.

1953: "We do not possess a systematic statement of the psychoanalytic theory of affects."

—David Rapaport (1953/1967, p. 476)

1987: Regarding affect, "Tomkins began a limited revolution—a paradigm shift, in Kuhnian terms."
—Peter Knapp (1987, p. 221)

1991: "Today we can turn to work of investigators of normal human development . . . for viable theories of affect, cognition, and learning."
—Michael Franz Basch (1991, pp. 294–95)

1991: "I continue to view affect as the primary innate biological motivating system."
—Silvan Tomkins (1991, p. 5)

2005: "[Freud] had no satisfactory hypothesis to account for affectivity in general . . . Adequate explanations of [affect] were finally proposed by Tomkins."
—John Gedo (2005, p. 90)

The Evolution of the Concept of Affects

The problem for those studying affects prior to the mid-1800s was a significant one, namely, the absence of data, especially data on infant and child development. For those readers who want a roadmap with which to begin exploring the earlier work in more depth, several sources do an admirable job of filling in this history from psychological, neurobiological, and philosophical perspectives (see, for example, Plutchik, 1962; Knapp, 1987; Tomkins, 1991; Panksepp, 1998, 2004; Cavell, 2003; Panksepp & Biven, 2012; Lear, 2015; Solms, 2021). The picture changed significantly in the second half of the 19th century with the arrival of Charles Darwin (1809–1882) and Sigmund Freud (1856–1939).

Darwin and Freud

In 1859, Charles Darwin's book on evolution was published: *On the Origin of Species by Means of Natural Selection, or the Preservation of Favoured Races in the Struggle for Life. Origin of Species* had very little discussion of *Homo sapiens*, however. Shortly thereafter, in 1862, the French neurologist G. B. Duchenne published his detailed mapping of the facial muscles. Darwin was influenced by and used many of Duchenne's findings. Darwin later concluded that certain human facial expressions and postures were built-in, inherited, universal responses that had evolved and ultimately formed a signaling and motivational system, that is, affects.

The relating of humans to evolution came in 1871, in *The Descent of Man, and Selection in Relation to Sex*. An early chapter in that book is titled "Comparison of the Mental Powers of Man and the Lower Animals." Darwin leaves no doubt about his intentions, saying, "My object in this chapter is to show that there is no fundamental difference between man and the higher mammals in their mental faculties" (1871, p. 35).

Photo 2.1 Charles Darwin
Source: Maull and Polyblank for the Literary and Scientific Portrait Club (1855)

Darwin's much lesser-known work, *The Expression of the Emotions in Man and Animals*, was first published in 1872. In it, Darwin discussed these specific responses and their evolutionary antecedents. He described a variety of human emotional expressions felt to be innate, inherited, and universal, including attention, joy, surprise, astonishment, anxiety, dejection, despair, sulkiness, anger, hatred, fear, horror, shame, shyness, contempt, and guilt. Darwin then described many of these expressions in our animal forebears, suggesting an evolutionary process.

Paul Ekman (1998) was responsible for the third edition of *Expression*, and he did a brilliant job of describing the remarkable advances Darwin made in understanding our affective world. Darwin also made a contribution to infant observation and research in his article "A Biographical Sketch of an Infant" (1877). Darwin thus points the way to an inherited, built-in system of emotional expressions and motivation. About a century later, Tomkins and his colleagues, together with infant researchers and neurobiologists, brought greater clarity to the way in which this affect system works (Basch, 1976, 1988; Gedo, 2005).

Prior to this, however, Sigmund Freud and his colleagues developed psychoanalysis. Gedo (2005) suggested Freud made four enduring scientific discoveries of major import: the development of the analytic observational method; the significance of the unconscious; the compulsion to repeat, i.e., transference and generalization; and the role of early childhood experiences. All four of these advances involve affects.

Influenced by Darwin and his theory of evolution, Freud initially considered affect to be "the conscious manifestation of instinct" (Basch, 1976, p. 771). Later,

Photo 2.2 Sigmund Freud
Source: Gift of Mr. Ernst Freud. Wellcome Collection 14091i

the concept of affect was conceived as part of an internal feedback system (Basch, 1976, p. 774; Freud, 1926, 1933). The psychoanalytic tradition has produced a huge literature on affect (e.g., David Rapaport, Henry Krystal, Henri Parens, Michael Franz Basch, Robert N. Emde, Daniel Stern, Arnold H. Modell, and others).

Beyond Darwin and Freud

By the middle of the 20th century, as described by Ekman (1998), anthropologists such as Margaret Mead, Gregory Bateson, and Ray Birdwhistell attempted to reject the inherited basis of emotional expression, arguing for cultural relativism. More recently, others have focused on emotions in adults to arrive at similar conclusions. Although cultural relativism appropriately looks at environmental effects on emotional expression, it tends to overlook studies of infants, their increasing capacity for voluntary affect expression with the development of the cortex, and the developmental integration of primary affects with learning and experience (Tomkins, 1991; Ekman, 1998). Consider how young children can intentionally change their expressions, often to manipulate a parent or caretaker, and how this becomes polished in an adult, for example, in actors and poker players. Current scientific data support the roles of evolutionary, inherited as well as environmental influences of expressions of emotion (e.g., Darwin, 1872b; Basch, 1976, 1988; Tomkins, 1991; Panksepp, 1998; Mayr, 2001; Demos, 2019).

Photo 2.3 Paul Ekman
Source: Courtesy of Paul Ekman

In the latter half of the 20th century, Tomkins and his colleagues advanced the understanding of affects by more specifically describing how they develop and function, their interactions with the environment, their roles in motivation as well as communication, and their clinical implications. Perhaps the best summary of this process is found in Tomkins's first two chapters of *Affect Imagery Consciousness, Volume III* (1991). Tomkins, Ekman, Carroll Izard, E. Virginia Demos, and Nathanson are leading proponents and developers of differential emotions theory, which takes its name from the emphasis on discrete emotions as distinct experiential/motivational processes. Basch (1976, 1988), Stern (1985), Demos (1995, 2019), Panksepp (1998), Gedo (2005), Holinger (2008, 2016), and others have supported these ideas from psychoanalytic, clinical, developmental, and neurobiological perspectives. Within differential emotions theory, there is a controversy regarding the number of discrete affects as well as the timing of their appearance in the infant (e.g., Ekman, 2003; Izard, 1977; Panksepp, 1998; Tomkins, 1991).

What Are the Various Affects?

In this book, nine primary affects are identified: two positive affects (interest, enjoyment), one resetting affect clearing the nervous system (surprise), and six negative affects (distress, anger, fear, shame, disgust [reaction to unpleasant tastes], and dissmell [reaction to unpleasant odors]). These operate on a scale of low-to-high: interest/excitement, enjoyment/joy, surprise/startle, distress/anguish, anger/rage, fear/terror, shame/humiliation, and lower and higher levels of disgust and dissmell.

Each affect is associated with specific skin, muscle, and autonomic responses (Table 2.1). The affects are conveyed through facial expressions, bodily movements,

Table 2.1 Nine Basic Affects and Some of Their Expressions

Affect	Manifestations
Interest to excitement	Eyebrows slightly lifted or slightly lowered
	Tracking
	Looking and listening
	Mouth may be a bit open
	Possible movement toward a target object
Enjoyment to joy	Smile
	Lips widened up and out
Surprise to startle	Eyebrows up
	Eyes open wide and blink
	Mouth open in O shape
Distress to anguish	Cry
	Arched eyebrows
	Corners of mouth turned down
	Tears
	Rhythmic sobbing
Anger to rage	Frown
	Eyes may be narrowed
	Clenched jaw
	Lips may be compressed or drawn back to expose teeth
	Red face
	Nostrils distended
	Neck muscles strained
Fear to terror	Eyes frozen open
	Pale
	Cold
	Sweaty
	Facial trembling with hair erect
Shame to humiliation	Lowering of eyelids
	Lowering of tonus of all facial muscles
	Lowering of the head via reduction in the tonus of neck muscles
	Unilateral tilting of the head in one direction
Disgust	Lower lip lowered and protruded
	Tongue protruded
Dissmell	Upper lip and nose raised
	Head turned away

and vocalizations. For example, surprise is marked by eyebrows up, eyes wide open, and mouth open in "O" shape. Distress is shown by arched eyebrows, corners of the mouth turned down, tears, rhythmic sobbing, and crying. Shame is expressed by lowering the head and tilting the head in one direction (Figure 2.1; for additional illustrations, see Holinger, 2003). The face (Figure 2.2) can be a particularly important source of the expression of affects—for infants, children, and adults—given the remarkable number of small muscles it contains (e.g., Darwin, 1872b; Tomkins, 1991; Ekman, 1973, 2003).

| Interest | Enjoyment | Surprise |

| Distress | Anger | Fear |

| Shame | Disgust | Dissmell |

Figure 2.1 Examples of affective responses

Source: "Interest," by permission of Chris and Ashley Holinger; "Surprise," by permission of Elise Cade; "Distress," photo by leungchopan; "Disgust," by permission of the Kim family; "Dissmell," photo by leungchopan; other photos © 2003 Paul C. Holinger, M.D.

Summarizing

This positive and negative quality of affects is the logical extension of Freud's proposals of affect theory (Basch, 1976; Gedo, 2005). In the years following

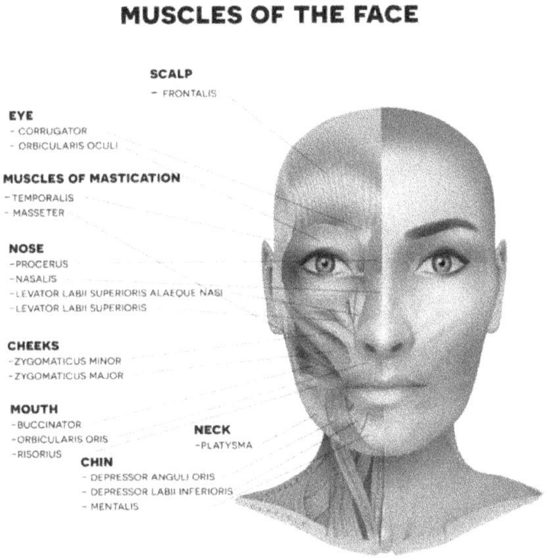

MUSCLES OF THE FACE

SCALP
- FRONTALIS

EYE
- CORRUGATOR
- ORBICULARIS OCULI

MUSCLES OF MASTICATION
- TEMPORALIS
- MASSETER

NOSE
- PROCERUS
- NASALIS
- LEVATOR LABII SUPERIORIS ALAEQUE NASI
- LEVATOR LABII SUPERIORIS

CHEEKS
- ZYGOMATICUS MINOR
- ZYGOMATICUS MAJOR

MOUTH
- BUCCINATOR
- ORBICULARIS ORIS
- RISORIUS

NECK
- PLATYSMA

CHIN
- DEPRESSOR ANGULI ORIS
- DEPRESSOR LABII INFERIORIS
- MENTALIS

Figure 2.2 Facial muscles

Freud's writings, the innovative works of various psychologists, psychoanalysts, and neurobiologists increased our understanding of affects and their mechanisms of action.

Peter Knapp once noted, "This literature encompasses a wide variety of definitions, approaches, and data . . . psychology as a whole speaks about emotion in many different tongues" (1987, pp. 205–206). Currently, most clinicians and scholars use the technical word *affect* for the earliest subcortical reactions to stimuli (Tomkins, 1962, 1991; Basch, 1976; Knapp, 1987; Izard, 1971; Demos, 1995; Ekman, 1998, 2003). That is how the term is used in this book. In this model, affects are distinct from the *physiologic drives* (e.g., hunger, thirst, sex, breathing) (Tomkins, 1991; Holinger, 2008). The affects are primary motivators and provide amplification to the drives (see Chapter 3).

With age, there are transformations from the biological to psychological: Affects combine with each other, with our experiences, learning, and various developmental changes to form our more complex emotional lives and nuances of feelings. For example, distress connected with a loss may produce what is called sadness. Affects integrate with cognition and language. Stern (1985), Lane and Schwartz (1987), Basch (1988), Tomkins (1991), and others have described these processes in various ways (e.g., see Holinger, 2003, pp. 249–251).

The terms *feelings* and *emotions* are often used in general to refer to emotional life beyond pure affect. Therefore, in this book, I will use feelings and emotions in their general meaning, i.e., beyond the subcortical affects. Others have used these two terms with reference to specific developmental periods. For example, Basch uses the term *feeling* as coming into being around 18–24 months, when the basic affective reactions are related to a concept of self. Emotion results when feeling states are joined with experience to give personal meaning to such concepts as love, hate, and happiness. Affective development that goes beyond the self-referential is considered empathic understanding (1988).

However, it should be noted that affects are retained throughout life. Humans can mask and alter their affective expressions from an early age (e.g., actors, poker players), but the underlying affects remain (Basch, 1988; Tomkins, 1991; see Chapter 3). It is interesting to note that Tomkins once attempted to create a dictionary of affects—words related to feelings and emotions. He finally abandoned the project, saying the number of words conveying the nuances of feelings in various languages was overwhelming.

In short, affects are seen as an innate stimulus-response signaling and motivational system consisting of approximately nine responses. In Chapter 3, I discuss how affects function in this model, and many examples are included.

Chapter 3

Current Concepts of Affects
Functions and Examples

Chapter Outline:
- How do affects function?
- Examples of affective responses
- Clinical implications and an illustration
- Manifestations of affects: A vignette
- Transformations of affects
- Summarizing: Some current concepts concerning the mechanisms of affects

The model of affects we are utilizing here, as conceptualized by Tomkins, suggests that humans are born with a stimulus-response signaling and motivational system initially consisting of approximately nine responses or affects. This stimulus-response system of affects combines with cognition and language and integrates with experience, learning, environmental influences, and brain maturation, resulting in our emotional life and development.

The nine affects are traditionally separated into positive and negative. Interest and enjoyment are considered positive affects. Distress, anger, fear, shame, disgust, and dissmell are negative affects. Surprise has been termed a resetting affect: It clears the assembly to create readiness for new stimuli. The outcome of surprise, then, depends on the affect following surprise.

Why are there more negative than positive affects? Perhaps given the helplessness of the neonate, it is more important to express danger signals, the SOS. However, this imbalance may be problematic, given the negative internalizations of affects that can occur during the early years via parenting and the environment.

This positive and negative bilateral valence of affects has been seen by some as the logical extension of Freud's proposals of affect theory (Basch, 1976; Gedo, 2005). With the later work of psychologists, psychoanalysts, and neurobiologists, affects and their mechanisms of action are much better defined and understood (Tomkins, 1962, 1991; Basch, 1976; Knapp, 1987; Ekman, 1998, 2003; Gedo, 2005; Panksepp & Bevin, 2012; de Waal, 2019; Lane & Nadel, 2020). These advances have enhanced our understanding of the assets, liabilities, and interactions of affects, cognition, and language in the personality development of human beings.

DOI: 10.4324/9780429203640-4

This knowledge, in turn, allows for greater clinical capacities to prevent problems and enhance potential. The power of affects, cognition, and language to shape individual happiness and society's well-being is far-reaching, and it can be utilized in both clinical work as well as in social policy.

The distinctions between positive and negative affects are important. For instance, education and learning can be enhanced by the positive affects of interest and enjoyment and impaired by the negative affects of anger, fear, and shame. Interest (curiosity) can fuel empathy and understanding. Mishandling of negative affects can inhibit interest and enjoyment and lead, for example, to two major social issues discussed later in the book—physical punishment and the problems associated with it (Chapter 12) and bias, prejudice, and violence (Chapter 13).

The concept of negative affects can also be useful in understanding trauma. *Trauma* can be defined as a disordered psychic or emotional state resulting from severe mental or emotional stress or physical injury. John Gedo provides an excellent summary of the history of trauma in his book *Psychoanalysis as Biological Science* (2005). Traumatic states can result from the loss of a parent or child, abusive parenting, the effects of war, sexual abuse, failures of various kinds, and so on—any might trigger negative affects to the point of trauma. However, the type and intensity of the trigger needed to create a traumatic state can vary dramatically from one individual to the next.

I would like to stress, however, that the term *negative affects* may be something of a misnomer in that these affects can be quite useful. In babies, the affects of distress, anger, and others are important signals to the environment that something is wrong and needs fixing. With age, a person can use negative affects to deal with issues in the environment (e.g., fear). And with the capacity for introspection, a person can utilize the affects of distress, shame, and so on to identify problems and make changes (Basch, 1988; Kelly & Lamia, 2018).

How Do Affects Function?

One of the most pressing questions about the nature of affects involves: How do affects function? And more specifically, how do biological drives, memory, imagination, thinking, words, and external stimuli all trigger a relatively small number of discrete responses called affects?

"Consider the nature of the problem," Tomkins (1991) wrote.

> The innate activators had to include the drives but not to be limited to them as exclusive activators. The neonate, for example, must respond with innate fear to any difficulty in breathing but must also be afraid of other objects.
>
> (p. 57)

The infant must be able to cry at hunger or a burn or cut or horrible taste. Each affect has to be activated, therefore, "by some general characteristic of neural stimulation, common to both internal and external stimuli and not too stimulus specific" (p. 57).

Photo 3.1 Silvan S. Tomkins
Source: Photograph by Irving Alexander

This model suggests that activation of innate affects involves *stimulation increase, stimulation level, and stimulation decrease*. Tomkins noted:

> I would account for the differences in affect activation by three variants of a single principle: the density of neural firing. By density I mean the frequency of neural firing per unit time. My theory posits three discrete classes of activators of affect, each of which further amplifies the sources which activate them. These are stimulation increase, stimulation level, and stimulation decrease.
>
> (1991, pp. 57–58)

In this model, Tomkins considers the nature of the external stimulus as well as the individual's unique response to the stimulus (via the density of the individual's internal neural firing).

For example, any stimulus (light, sound, etc.) with a relatively sudden onset and a steep increase in the rate of neural firing will innately activate a surprise response. If the rate increases less rapidly, fear is activated. If the rate increases still less rapidly, then interest is innately activated. With the slower rate of neural firing, the result will be interest rather than surprise or fear (Figure 3.1). (See Examples #1 and #4 further on).

In contrast, any sustained increase in the quantity of neural firing (such as a continuing loud noise) would innately activate the cry of distress. If it were sustained and still louder, it would activate the anger response (Figure 3.2).

Any sudden decrease in stimulation that reduces the rate of neural firing, such as in the sudden reduction of excessive noise, would innately activate the smile of enjoyment. In everyday language, there is a decrease in tension, resulting in enjoyment (Figure 3.3).

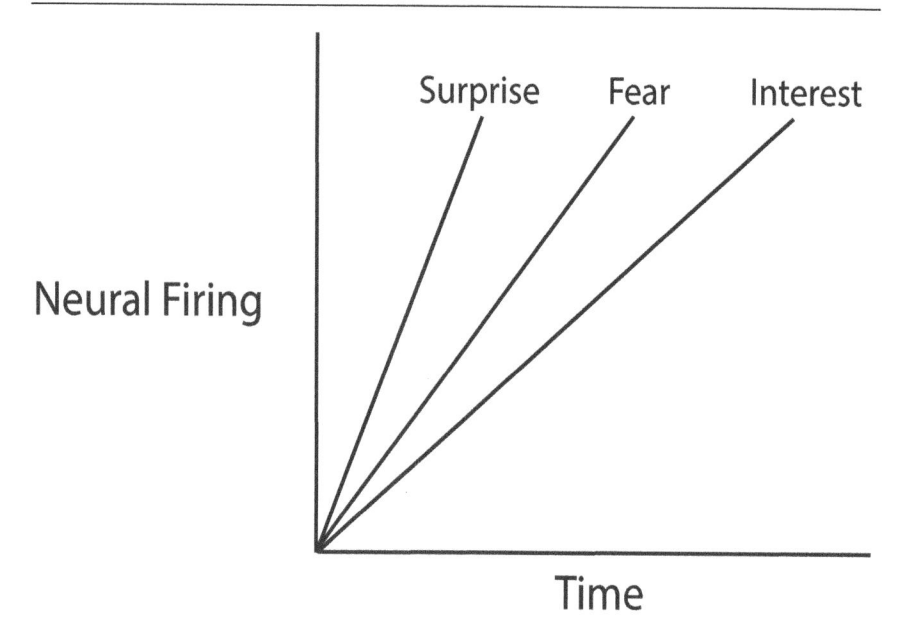

Figure 3.1 Any stimulus with a relatively sudden onset and a steep increase in the rate of neural firing will innately activate surprise. If the rate increases less rapidly, fear is activated. If the rate increases even less rapidly, interest is innately activated.

Thus, the affects of surprise, fear, interest, and enjoyment are related to the gradient (increase or decrease) of the stimulus, whereas distress and anger are related to the quantity of the stimulus.

The affects of shame, disgust, and dissmell are similar to, but different from, the six innate affects described in the preceding paragraphs. There exists a large body of literature on shame (e.g., Morrison, 1989; Nathanson, 1992; Lansky & Morrison, 1997; Kelly & Lamia, 2018). Shame is specifically related to other affects.

- Shame is triggered by an interference with or an inhibition of interest and enjoyment. It involves a mismatch between the expectations and hopes of the infant (or individual) and the response of the caregiver (or environment). Shame operates after the affects of interest or enjoyment have been activated; it impedes one or the other or both. Shame is an inhibitor of continuing interest and enjoyment.
- In addition, shame, shyness, guilt, and discouragement may have the same core affect, although experienced due to different perceived causes and consequences: Shame is about inferiority; shyness is about the strangeness of the other; guilt is about moral transgression; and discouragement is about temporary defeat.

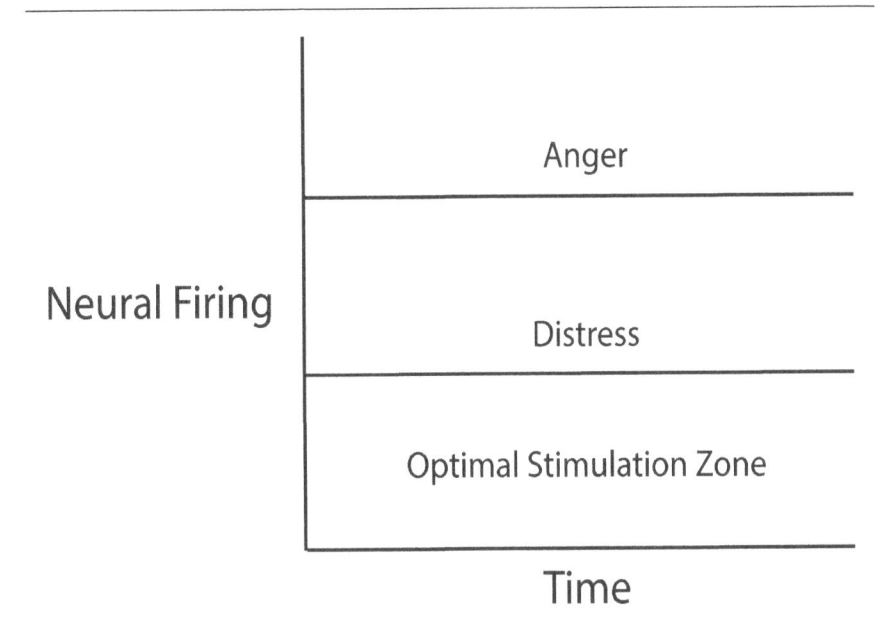

```
                    |
                    |
                    |  Anger
                    |_____
Neural Firing       |
                    |  Distress
                    |_____
                    |
                    |  Optimal Stimulation Zone
                    |_____
                           Time
```

Figure 3.2 Any sustained increase in the level of neural firing, such as continuing loud noise, innately activates the cry of distress. If it were sustained and still louder, it would innately activate the anger response.

- Shame also appears intimately related to self-esteem. The development of a healthy sense of self and self-esteem involves validation of the positive affects of interest and enjoyment and concepts of competency (e.g., Basch, 1988; Knapp, 1987; Kohut, 1971; Stern, 1985). The inappropriate and excessive use of shame thus erodes self-esteem inasmuch as it interferes with the positive affects.

Disgust and dissmell are considered to be innate defensive responses. Their function is to protect the human from noxious and dangerous foods and odors.

- *Disgust* is related to taste and the gastrointestinal system; nausea and vomiting can be elicited to help rid the body of dangerous substances.
- *Dissmell* involves the olfactory system, with the typical evasive maneuvers visible in infancy. The early warning response via the nose is dissmell; the next level of response, from the mouth or stomach, is disgust.
- Later, these two affects are related psychologically to rejection and contempt, respectively. Such phrases as "this leaves a bad taste in my mouth" or "this has a bad smell to it" convey the link between the physiological affects of disgust and dissmell and psychological rejection and contempt.

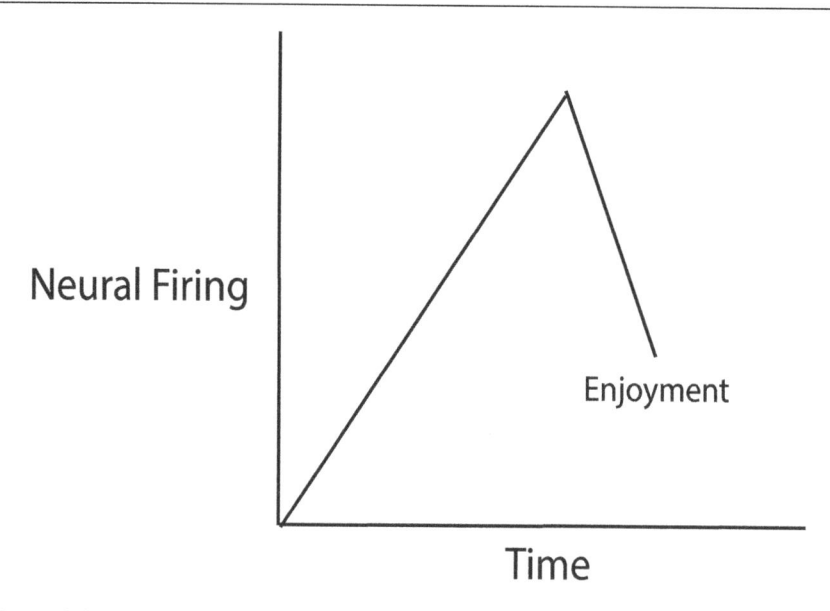

Figure 3.3 Any sudden decrease in neural firing, as in the sudden reduction of excessive noise, would innately activate the smile of enjoyment.

Jennifer Lock Oman, psychotherapist and social worker, calls disgust and dismell "emotions of distance" in that they contribute to distancing from one another (personal communication). These affects are also important aspects of bias and prejudice (see Chapter 13). In addition to being directed outward at others, these affects can also be directed inward and .be self-denigrating and indicative of negative self-states—e.g., "I am disgusting" and "I stink."

In this model, affects can be seen as primary motivators and as providing amplification, including the physiologic drives (e.g., hunger, thirst, sex, breathing) (Tomkins, 1981). Without amplification of the affect system, "nothing else matters—and with its amplification, anything else *can* matter. It lends its power to memory, to perception, to thought, and to action no less than to the drives" (Tomkins, 1991, p. 6, emphasis in the original). The drives need amplification of affect in order to function. For example:

> Sexuality, in order to become possible, must borrow its potency from the affect of excitement. The drive must be assisted by an *amplifier* if it is to work at all. Freud, better than anyone else, knew that the blind, pushy, imperious Id was the most fragile of impulses readily disrupted by fear, by shame, by rage, by boredom. At the first sign of affect *other* than excitement, there is impotence

and frigidity. The penis proves to be a paper tiger in the absence of appropriate affective amplification.

(Tomkins, 1991, p. 6, emphasis in original)

Affects also interact with themselves in various ways and can be innate activators of other affects. For example, anger can be triggered by distress as well as by an excessively sustained level of the other negative affects (fear, shame, disgust, dissmell) or positive affects (e.g., too-long-sustained excitement); the interruption of interest can lead to distress, and then anger; and shame is a specific inhibitor of continuing interest and enjoyment. Furthermore, affects themselves may act as regulators and modulators of other affects. For instance, activation of the positive affect of interest can diminish fear and distress (Taylor et al., 1997; Tomkins, 1963). See Example #2.

Tomkins suggests that this affect model is an innate system, a primary motivator. It also takes into account an individual's unique responses to certain stimuli as well as the capacity to learn. Affects and learning become intertwined. Infants can learn very quickly from the environment (caregivers) what is to be feared and what is of interest. This learning can be done through nonverbal and verbal sources and also formal education. This early learning itself can change later with development and experience.

For example, a remark or noise may rattle one person and not another. This may be due to inborn individual differences or learning and experience: A sudden loud noise of an airplane close overhead might startle someone not used to airplanes

Photo 3.2 Various affects are visible on the faces of the spectators as an angry baseball player throws a chair into the stands

Source: Photographer: D. Ross Cameron

Photo 3.3 Richard D. Lane
Source: Courtesy of Richard D. Lane

but not bother another who lives close to an airport. As Susanne Langer notes, the intensity of the stimulus may not be equivalent to the effect (1967, p. 284)—that is, individual differences may be either inborn or learned. In addition, infants and young children, as well as adults, can quickly learn to alter their facial expressions in response to specific stimuli (see Example # 3).

This concept of affects posits them as a stimulus-response, information processing system, consistent with recent neurophysiological studies. As Gedo (2005) noted, "In other words, affectivity becomes a cybernetic system of intrapsychic communication" (pp. 90–91). Tomkins laid the groundwork for understanding affects, and since his death, the bulk of recent neurophysiologic research has tended to support the basic idea of innate affects. Various authors, including Richard Lane, have adroitly summarized the burgeoning studies documenting the roles of the brainstem, limbic system, and neocortex in the development, processing, and regulation of the affective processes (e.g., Damasio, 2003; George et al., 1995; Panksepp, 1998; Paradiso et al., 1997; Reiman et al., 1997; Schore, 1994; Taylor et al., 1997; Lane & Nadel, 2020).

Examples of Affective Responses

The following are some everyday-life examples, followed by a clinical illustration with a focus on affect. Additional clinical examples can be found in Chapters 5 and 11.

Example #1

Recently, I was at a sports arena near an airport. As several very young children were approaching the arena, suddenly, there was a tremendously loud noise! The youngsters first showed a startle response, then quickly the fear response, and then, as they began to realize what it was—an airplane had appeared from just behind the arena as it approached its landing—they showed an interest response.

Example #2

The following example shows how the expression of affects—the biological reactions to stimuli—can be very rapid. I remember playing once with a little one-and-a-half-year-old girl. She was quite tired, but she was also fascinated by the ball we were rolling and bouncing back and forth. The affects literally flickered across her face—interest, surprise, enjoyment, and distress. The rapidity and visibility of the affects were amazing—the surprise and interest and enjoyment expressions in a very rapid succession when we bounced the ball together, and the distress when the ball was not being bounced.

Example #3

High-speed films reveal how affects and their expressions are retained into adulthood. These films show that even when adults try consciously to suppress expressions of certain affects (for example, distress and anger following a slightly painful stimulus), the biological reactions can still be briefly seen on the face. Thus, the innate biological reactions to stimuli are still visible in adulthood, even when experience and development in the cerebral cortex lead to greater conscious control over the expression of feelings. Consider the poker player, actor, or politician who tries to control their feelings under various circumstances. In this process, with age, the capacity of the cortex allows for increasing control over expressions as well as increased reason over actions and behaviors.

Example #4

I was out walking in our neighborhood when I was startled by a loud noise nearby and slightly behind me—whoos, whoos, whuff, whuff . . . I was startled, then scared, and I could feel a tingling through my neck and body . . . the image of a hawk with its wings beating flashed through my mind. I turned quickly around—and then saw near me a person trying to start a motorcycle. In just this second or two, I could feel the surprise, the fear, then interest as I began to process that the noise was coming from the motorcycle.

Clinical Implications and an Illustration

Over the past several decades, there has been an increased emphasis on earlier developmental issues (including affects), e.g., preoedipal/oedipal distinctions, noninterpretive and interpretive interventions, object-relations theories, relational models, self-psychology, and so on (see Winnicott, 1965a; Kohut, 1971; Modell,

1976; Gedo, 1979; Bacal & Newman, 1990; Holinger, 1989, 1999). In this book, I hope to convey that an enhanced understanding of affect can be useful in a variety of developmental and clinical situations. Tomkins nicely frames the roles and potential benefits of understanding affects in clinical work:

> Psychopathology is much too complex to yield to simple remedies. I am not suggesting that an understanding of the innate activating mechanism (affects) ... is sufficient to enable the cure of neurosis or psychosis ... Nonetheless, "interpretation" psychotherapy *without* knowledge of or attention to the nature of the innate activating mechanism is as blind as any other kind of unconsciousness. The finer the texture of understanding of the complexities of psychological processes, the more effective therapeutic procedures can become. *Interpretation will be radically enriched if it is embedded in an understanding of the causal matrix of the innate affect-activating mechanism.*
>
> (Tomkins, 1991, p. 147, italics added)

The case study of Dr. B provides one illustration of how a focus on affect may be beneficial.

Case Study: Dr. B

Dr. B contacted a consultant for help with a twice-a-week psychotherapy case she had started some months prior. The patient, Ms. N, was a recently divorced 28-year-old secretary whose life was characterized by emotional volatility, storms of anger and sadness, and somewhat erratic relationships. The major problem that led Ms. N to seek treatment was the situation with her ex-husband: She continued to have very painful and disruptive feelings for and contact with him six months after his leaving and divorcing her.

Dr. B described the first several months of treatment as focused primarily on Ms. N's distressing on-again, off-again contacts with her ex-husband. Mr. N would contact his ex-wife, manage to bring her into his emotional orbit again, and then reject and disappoint her in some way. Within this context, Dr. B addressed a variety of issues with her patient over the first several months, using what she described as an interpretive framework with a focus on the transference. These interventions included highlighting the patient's apprehension about beginning treatment, her difficulties trusting the therapist, and the various displacements and resistances involved; exploring the possibility that the patient's distressing feelings for and interactions with her ex-husband were reflections of aspects of her early object relations; and working on the self-destructive and possibly defensive nature of Ms. N's not extricating herself from these disruptive contacts with her ex-husband. Although the patient appeared to settle into therapy and consider her therapist's interpretations, after months, nothing much seemed to change—neither the patient's painful intrapsychic world nor her erratic, disruptive interpersonal relationships.

It was at this point that Dr. B sought consultation. Her consultant made what seemed to be a deceptively simple observation and suggestion. In short, she suggested a focus on Ms. N's affect and current object of that affect, namely, how it was so horribly painful—distressing, embarrassing, humiliating—still to be wrapped up so intensely and erratically with her ex-husband and not be able to break away or resolve it somehow. As she shifted the nature of her interventions over the following weeks, Dr. B noted that Ms. N seemed to respond much more positively to treatment. Ms. N described a feeling of being better understood and a sense of relief; she began tearfully elaborating on her feelings for her ex-husband, the pros and cons of that relationship, and her sense of loss, and she appeared to begin a mourning process, and her disruptive behavior, including with her ex-husband, began to dissipate. The process continued in this fashion for the next several months; that is, the changes in the therapist's stance and the patient's response persisted. Ms. N noted her sense that "now we're getting somewhere," and Dr. B felt the process was deepening in that Ms. N seemed to be communicating more freely and expressing her affects more openly and directly.

Several months later, Dr. B noted gradual changes, at first subtle and then more apparent, in Ms. N's talking manner; namely, Ms. N appeared to be increasingly self-reflective and curious. She seemed more insightful about her subjective states and the internal and external precipitants of her feelings and actions. Interestingly, Ms. N herself now began to inquire about and explore the kind of issues and questions Dr. B had raised at the beginning of treatment. Dr. B noted how Ms. N appeared to respond more psychologically-mindedly and productively (internally and externally) to the interpretive nature of these interventions, interactions that, in retrospect, seemed counterproductive at the beginning of treatment.

To summarize, in this case, I have tried to highlight the potential of one variable—affect—in the midst of a complicated clinical situation. In the vignette to follow, Tomkins describes a parent-child interaction that emphasizes the impact of negative affects on development.

Manifestations of Affects: A Vignette

We turn now from the clinical case to an example of affects in action in the midst of child development. In the following fictional vignette, Tomkins presents a series of everyday-type interactions between a little boy and his parents. He describes several exchanges that include various affective reactions, focusing particularly on the disruptive and debilitating aspects of shame (Tomkins, 1963, pp. 228–230).

Our hero is a child who is destined to have every affect totally bound by shame. We see him first with his age equals. He is a friendly, somewhat timid child who is being bullied. He is not angry with the bully; indeed, he is a little afraid of him. His reluctance to fight evokes taunts of "sissy," "chicken," and "yellow" from those who themselves may be shamed by this timidity. Rather than tolerate his shame, he will permit himself to be coerced into flying in the face of fear and fight the dreaded bully.

The same timid one, coerced into tolerating fear by his age equals and into fighting the bully, may return home to be shamed into mortification for having fought. "Nice little boys don't fight like ruffians. Mother is ashamed of you. Whatever got into you? You know better than that."

The timid one may now start to cry in distress. The feeling of shame has passed a critical density and tears well up in the eyes and add to the intensity of his sobbing. At this point, his father, attracted by the childlike, even effeminate display of tears, expresses manly contempt for such weakness: "What are you crying for, like a two-year-old? Stop it—you make me sick."

Our hero stops crying and sits down with his family for dinner. The first course is a fruit cup, which he detests. Rather than unobtrusively putting it aside, he lifts his upper lip and gives every manifestation of struggling with overwhelming nausea. He is disgusted and has given the customary biological sign of this affect. Both parents immediately fight fire with fire. Disgust is opposed by disgust, calculated not to express rejection of food but to arouse shame intense enough to inhibit the disgust reaction in their pride and joy. "Don't ever make that face again at the table—it is disgusting—you don't see us making such expressions, do you?"

The child subsides with his head bent low until the next course, which is roast beef—his favorite food. His excitement overflows into action. "I love roast beef," he blurts out as he reaches across the table to pull off a small, weakly attached sliver from the end of the roast. Father's nostrils and lip lift, the boy's name is emitted in tones saturated with revulsion. The offending hand is withdrawn, the eyes lowered, their excitement contained.

After an eternity of waiting, the beef is before him. His excitement is confirmed. It does taste as good as he expected. He shouts his joy so that the neighborhood and the larger community may share in his delight, "Oh, boy! This is good!"

This time Mother defends the elementary decencies upon which Western civilization rests: "Oh Robert, you'd think you hadn't eaten in a week, really!" Father's eyes reinforce the message till the joy is contained and the head drops in shame. Dinner proceeds uneventfully until both parents become uncomfortably aware that their dinner companion is endangering their appetite by the removal of his face from view and by the limpness of his posture, suggestive of complete surrender to the affect of shame.

Our vignette draws to a close with shame turned against shame: "Robert, where are your manners? Sit up. It's not polite to sit like that at the dinner table." Robert sits up with face and limbs wooden lest they betray shame. The parents are temporarily appeased, but eventually, the apathy and listlessness of their child becomes distressing. In the final scene, shame is turned against apathy: "Robert, you could be a little more attentive, you don't have to sit there like a lump on a log. Say something."

So our hero is taught that the affect per se is shameful, that shame itself is caught up in the same taboo, and that even affect-lessness may be shameful.

It is not uncommon to see and hear these types of affective interchanges as we go about our daily routines, although not in such a concentrated form. Thus, in this vignette, Tomkins is illustrating the power not only of shame but of all negative affects to disrupt one's sense of self.

Transformations of Affects

Tomkins and his colleagues suggested the term *General Images* for the "centrally generated blueprint which controls the human feedback system" (1963, p. 261). This consists of four aspects: *Maximize positive affect; minimize negative affect (the causes, not expression); minimize affect inhibition; and maximize the power to maximize positive affect to minimize negative affect and to minimize affect inhibition.* As I will show in more detail throughout this book, these principles help explain much of what is beneficial in understanding and transforming affects.

For example, Marie Curie's famous quote highlights her grappling with the tension between fear and curiosity and the shift from fear to interest: "Nothing in life is to be feared, it is only to be understood. Now is the time to understand more, so that we may fear less."

In development and parenting, we want to enhance and validate the infant's sense of interest (curiosity) and enjoyment and minimize distress, fear, and shame due to the toxicity and trauma involved. With respect to interpersonal skills, a focus on positive affects tends to lead readily to behavioral change and avoids the contagious and toxic nature of, for example, anger and fear.

The clinical arena is also at issue here: Psychotherapy concerns efforts to understand causes of negative affects (e.g., anger, fear, shame) and enhance the capacity for positive affects (interest and enjoyment). The therapist works to navigate various conscious and unconscious defenses, e.g., repression, disavowal, and others. As Freud (1915), Basch (1988), and others have noted, defense is always directed against affect, highlighting the centrality of emotional life. Interpretive work and the therapeutic relationship aim at understanding the negative aspects of the internal world and external behaviors and enhancement of positive affects of interest and enjoyment.

Self-understanding also involves an affective transformation by increasing the capacity for interest (curiosity and ultimately a self-analytic function) and understanding what one truly likes and does not like—crucial in the choice of friends, partner, and career. As Gedo noted, one of the most useful aspects of therapy is helping patients understand and "overcome any denial of their vulnerability to stress" (2005, p. 168). As I will show in more detail throughout this book, these principles help explain much of what is beneficial in understanding and transforming affects.

Summarizing: Some Current Concepts Concerning the Mechanisms of Affects

There has been much discussion about the nature of affects in various scientific disciplines. Here, I will review some of the perspectives supported by clinical and other data.

- First, the models of Freud and Tomkins noted here have interesting similarities. Both have a binary notion of the subjective experience of affect (positive and negative). Tomkins substantiates Freud's ideas of pleasure and unpleasure in demonstrating the positive and negative aspects of the various affects, notions that are supported by neurophysiologic research (e.g., Panksepp). The difference lies in Tomkins's further elaboration of the number of types of affects and the proposed mechanisms of action. Another example involves the drives. Both, as I have discussed, retain the idea of drives, but for Tomkins, affects are amplifiers of drives and, hence, more the motivating agents.
- Second, Tomkins's ideas include an explicit focus on both the internal world and the environment. This has several implications. It addresses the development of our more complex emotional life, as affects interact with each other as well as with the environment and experience. The environment is taken into account in that affects are biological responses to different kinds of external and internal stimuli.

    The response of the organism depends on the gradient and quantity of stimuli. The internal world is taken into account in that each individual has optimal stimulation levels of density of neural firing needed to trigger the affects; that is, individual temperament comes into play (e.g., Thomas & Chess, 1977): Each person has their own threshold for stimulation. In addition, the explicit bilateral focus (internal world and environment) is consistent with object-relations concepts and current clinical ideas involved with two-person psychology as well as with clinical work with children and adults that have to take both the internal world and environment into account.

    The ongoing debate about the influence of nature and nurture accounts for how psychoanalytic theories seem to oscillate over time between an emphasis on the internal world, on the one hand, and the role of the environment, on the other. The individual internal capacities of the organism (the intrapsychic), as well as the rapidity and level of the stimulus (environment), are both taken into account.
- Third, these ideas suggest further understanding of transference in the clinical situation. With development and life experiences, the affective triggering system becomes altered and expanded by learning and meaning. Learned activators of affects may include objects, words, imagination, and other affects. Language itself can both express affect and trigger affect. Various stimuli can trigger the same primary affects. Combinations of affects and experiences give subtlety and shadings to later emotional life. For example, Tomkins (1963) considered sadness a variation of distress in which the experience of loss was involved with the eliciting of distress.

- Fourth, Tomkins's script theory explores how affects integrate with each other and experience. *Script theory* represents the manifestation of these ideas about affect in developmental and clinical processes (Tomkins, 1991, 1992). Script theory accounts for the role of the affect in character structure. "In script theory, I define the scene as the basic element in life as it is lived . . . [It] includes at least one affect and at least one object of that affect" (Tomkins, 1991, p. 74). The object is not necessarily a person and may even be another affect. Connecting one affect-laden scene with another affect-laden scene involves the formation of scripts. The script deals with the individual's rules for predicting, interpreting, responding to, and controlling a set of scenes. Major affective scripts include affluent scripts, damage-reparation scripts, limitation-remediation scripts, decontamination scripts, anti-toxic scripts, and affect-management scripts (Tomkins, 1991; Demos, 1995, 2019; Nathanson, 1996; Kelly & Lamia, 2018).
- Fifth, Tomkins's model currently reframes the ideas of J. Bowlby, P. Fonagy, and other attachment theorists regarding a specific attachment drive. Rather, affects are seen to underlie aspects of attachment, and attachment is mediated by affects. As Demos (1989) stated,

> attachment theory as represented in the works of Bowlby (1969), Ainsworth et al. (1978), Sroufe and Waters (1977). . . argues that there is a preorganized behavioral, emotional, perceptual system specialized for attachment which has been inherited from our primate ancestors and is designed to decrease the physical distance between the infant and the caregiver in time of danger. By contrast, the view presented here [that is, Tomkins and colleagues] speaks of highly organized and coordinated systems that the infant has inherited from evolutionary processes but conceptualized these systems at a more basic and general level, for example, the perceptual, cognitive, affective, motor, and homeostatic systems, which are designed to function equally well in the inanimate or animate world, and in safe as well as dangerous moments.
>
> (p. 293)

In this chapter, I discussed affects and various aspects of their functioning. It is now time to turn to what may be our most important affect, that of interest.

Chapter 4

The Affect of Interest
The Core of Our Existence

Chapter Outline:

- Some essentials
- Evolution of our understanding of interest
- Interest and enjoyment
- Children and interest
- Understanding, sharing, and validating a child's interest
- Enhancing interest: Bret, *Green Eggs and Ham*, Carl
- Interfering with interest

Interest is a positive affect of great importance. It underlies our learning and exploratory activities. At its most intense, it becomes excitement.

The enhancement or inhibition of the affect of interest is one of the most important issues in human development facing caregivers and clinicians. It has profound implications for development, character structure, and treatment. When it is supported and encouraged, it expands curiosity and emotional and factual information, and it promotes greater adaptive capacities in new situations. As the child psychoanalyst Helen Beiser wrote, "Curiosity is a powerful motivating force in human behavior . . . it can be a powerful force in work and creativity, as well as a lot of fun" (1984, pp. 517, 525). Even Albert Einstein (1952) claimed to "have no special talent. I am only passionately curious." When curiosity is inhibited, positive and growth-supporting new learning is less likely.

Some Essentials

- The human brain is an information processing system. The responses of caregivers to infants and children can either enhance interest or constrict it. Similarly, later in life, family, friends, teachers, and employers can stimulate or restrict interest and curiosity.
- In terms of development and character structure, enhanced interest allows for increased learning, discovery, creativity, and adaptability to changing circumstances (Beiser, 1984).

- Clinically, one of the most important accomplishments a therapist can achieve in psychoanalysis and psychotherapy is helping a patient find increased interest and curiosity about his or her motives, behaviors, and relationships to the external world, in other words, their self-reflective capacities. "As Gardiner (1983) was the first to note, even the traditional technique of psychoanalysis works only insofar as it trains the analysand to perform effective self-inquiry" (Gedo, 2005, pp. 168–169).
- The impact of inhibited interest in childhood can have a profound ripple effect on the individual and society (e.g., it nurtures bias and prejudice). But the transformation of affects such as fear, surprise, and disgust into interest enhances learning and understanding.

Despite its importance, Tomkins noted interest is "that affect which has been most seriously neglected" (1962, p. 337). Fortunately, there appears to be greater focus recently on the affect of interest in both the psychoanalytic (e.g., Akhtar, 2017) and general literature (e.g., Pink, 2009; Gray, 2013). There is a growing awareness that interest underlies concepts such as play, creativity, learning, and changing. There is also an appreciation of what happens to an individual when interest is stifled by shame or fear, as we saw with Robert in the vignette in Chapter 3—boredom, depression, and various interferences with development and potentials (e.g., Morrison, 1989; Nathanson, 1992; Kelly & Lamia, 2018).

Evolution of Our Understanding of Interest

Darwin was known for his limitless interest in wide-ranging topics and almost insatiable curiosity.

> I have no great quickness of apprehension or wit . . . My power to follow a long and purely abstract train of thought is very limited . . . I think that I am superior . . . in noticing things which easily escape attention, and in observing them carefully . . . What is far more important, my love of natural science has been steady and ardent.
>
> (1881, p. 43)

In *The Expression of the Emotions in Man and Animals* (1872), he explored the revolutionary concept that there were demonstrable similarities between the emotional expressions of humans and animals. He showed clearly how animals seem to manifest expressions of what we now call affects: fear, distress, anger, disgust, and enjoyment, among others.

However, upon first reading, he appears to have said little overtly about curiosity or interest; neither word is even listed in his 1872 index. Indeed, Tomkins stated that Darwin missed the affect of interest: "The affect of interest or excitement is, paradoxically, absent from Darwin's catalogue of emotions. Although Darwin dealt with surprise and meditation the more sustained affect of interest per se was somehow overlooked" (1962, p. 337).

I do not entirely agree with Tomkins on this point. In 1872, Darwin does use the term *attention* to refer to what might be considered the affect of interest. When speaking of dogs, he noted, "[I]f his attention be suddenly aroused, he instantly pricks his ears to listen" (Darwin, 1872b; Ekman, 1998, p. 283). Darwin then turned to humans:

> When the attention is concentrated for a length of time with fixed earnestness on any object or subject, all the organs of the body are forgotten and neglected . . . Therefore, many of the muscles tend to become relaxed, and the jaw drops from its own weight . . . Or again, if our attention continues long and earnestly absorbed, all our muscles become relaxed, and the jaw, which was at first suddenly opened, remains dropped. Thus, several causes concur towards this same movement, whenever surprise, astonishment or amazement is felt.
>
> (p. 284)

To put these passages in context, it should be noted that Darwin here is wrestling with why the mouth is open during surprise. He considers such possibilities as increased hearing, increased breathing capacity, and relaxation of the jaw muscles.

From the modern perspective, what Darwin has described is the affect of interest, with the mouth being open somewhat. Furthermore, even earlier, in *The Descent of Man* (1871), Darwin was quite explicit about "curiosity," as shown in this delightful vignette:

> We will now turn to the more intellectual emotions and faculties, which are very important, as forming the basis for the development of the higher mental powers. Animals manifestly enjoy excitement and suffer from ennui, as may be seen with dogs, and, according to Rengger, with monkeys. All animals feel **Wonder**, and many exhibit **Curiosity**. They sometimes suffer from this latter quality, as when the hunter plays antics and thus attracts them; I have witnessed this with deer, and so it is with the wary chamois, and with some kinds of wild-ducks. Brehm gives a curious account of the instinctive dread, which his monkeys exhibited, for snakes; but their curiosity was so great that they could not desist from occasionally satiating their horror in a most human fashion, by lifting up the lid of the box in which the snakes were kept.
>
> (Darwin, *The Descent of Man*, 1871, 2nd Edition, 1874, p. 73, emphasis in original)

Thus, Darwin clearly described interest to some extent as "attention" and "curiosity" in relationship to surprise, astonishment, and amazement. However, it was up to his successors to explicitly describe the manifestations of interest-excitement, its mode of action, and its importance. It is to these successors I now turn.

Tomkins is very clear about the importance of interest. "It is interest . . . which is primary," he wrote. Interest "supports both what is necessary for life and what is possible" (1962, pp. 342, 345). Carroll Izard, an early collaborator of Tomkins, has also written an overlooked, wonderfully detailed discussion of the history and significance of interest (1977).

Tomkins suggests interest is closely related to surprise and fear:

> Any stimulus with a relatively sudden onset and a steep increase in the rate of neural firing will innately activate a startle response . . . if the rate of neural firing increases less rapidly, fear is activated; and if still less rapidly, the interest is innately activated.
>
> (1991, p. 58)

So, a sudden, unexpected gunshot will usually evoke surprise rather than interest. However, the individual's perceptual system and threshold for stimulation are also important in determining the rate of internal neural firing. Depending on circumstances, experience, and temperament, a gunshot might trigger fear or interest instead of surprise. In this formulation, both the extrinsic and intrinsic aspects of the stimulus-response system are addressed.

Age and experience are among the factors influencing affective patterns: The older the human being, the more experience is linked up with specific stimulus-response patterns. What matters, then, is not just the speed and quantity of the stimuli but the perceptual system with which that stimulus interacts. There are two clinical implications involved here. The first involves the processes underlying transferences, including patient/therapist, parent/child, spouse/spouse, student/supervisor, employee/employer, and so on. Stern's Representations of Interactions, which have been Generalized (RIGs) (1985), and Tomkins's script theory (1991) fall into this category. The second concerns the importance of early therapy—child and adolescent psychotherapy and analysis.

Neurobiology also has a place in this discussion. Exciting research by many talented scientists has been conducted on the neurobiology of emotions. Names such as Damasio, Lane, LeDoux, Panksepp, and Schore are among them. This type of research has tended to support the idea of primary (innate or categorical) affects, that is, biological substrates that mediate feeling states such as fear, anger, distress . . . and interest.

Jaak Panksepp (1998, 2004) has done an excellent job of integrating the information on animal models with the interest affect. He coined the term *SEEKING system* (the capital letters are his) to refer to the feeling of interest or curiosity. Panksepp contended that the "SEEKING system appears to control appetitive activation—the search, foraging, and investigatory activities—that all animals must exhibit before they are in a position to emit consummatory behaviors" (1998, p. 146). Panksepp suggested research shows that the SEEKING system is mediated by dopamine circuits, in particular, the medial forebrain bundle of the lateral hypothalamus. This psychobehavioral state can be evoked with localized brain stimulation in this area.

Photo 4.1 Jaak Panksepp
Source: Henry Moore Jr/Washington State University

Interest and Enjoyment

There is an intriguing relationship between interest and enjoyment. Enjoyment is triggered by a relatively steep reduction of the density of neural firing. Tomkins suggested:

> In the case of pain, fear and distress, the smile of joy is a smile of relief. In the case of sudden anger reduction, it is the smile of triumph. The same principle operates with the sudden reduction of pleasure, as after the orgasm or completion of a good meal, there is often the smile of pleasure.
>
> (1962, p. 371)

Interest and enjoyment can oscillate rapidly. For example, say you are working on an interesting project. There will usually be a series of oscillations between the interest in novel ideas and the enjoyment of thinking them through and solving problems. So long as a combination of new ideas and solutions continues, your interest will remain alive. When you run out of new possibilities, you will lose interest (Tomkins, 1962). In addition, enjoyment can be activated by anticipation of what has previously caused excitement.

The positive affects of interest and enjoyment are also crucial in modulating the late nights, the fatigue, etc., which are often required to complete a big project, a degree, a trial, and so on. The interest involved may be in the content of the project or in the positive outcomes accompanying completion, such as a degree, pay raise, or honor. If interest is not sufficient, it may be difficult to overcome the negative affects of distress, fear, anger, and shame. As noted by the child analyst Claudia Lament, the negative affects interfering with the completion of a "big project" may involve several dynamics, such as fear of not being up to the task, fragile self-esteem regulation, identifications with underperforming parents, and sadomasochistic rewards for not finishing the work (personal communication, 2021).

The reciprocal interaction of the positive affects of interest and enjoyment can be seen to be at the root of sustained interest—our careers, relationships, and so on. As Tomkins noted, "The reciprocal interplay between excitement and enjoyment is of critical significance in the creation of . . . long-term commitments" (1962, p. 368).

We can also see the relationship between interest and enjoyment in the milliseconds that it takes for an infant to express affects. Suppose a baby sees a face. Depending on past experience and the rapidity of the appearance of the face, surprise or fear might emerge first. Then, perhaps interest would be seen, and if the face is familiar and not scary, you will see the smile of enjoyment because of the reduction of fear or interest as the information processing ceases. These relationships between enjoyment, pattern-matching, the associated decrease in tension, and concepts of order and coherence will be discussed more fully later when prejudice and anger are explored. Similarly, humor provides another example. It is the sudden unexpectedness of the punchline that both surprises and terminates, further increasing information processing.

Children and Interest

Young babies have a special interest in faces. The human face seems to be an innate stimulus for the infant's interest. The infant will focus on a face over other options. Not only that, but research shows the baby will spend the most time looking at the eyes and the second-most time looking at the mouth. This may be due to the importance of the facial-signaling system itself. There are many small muscles in the face that make up the facial-signaling system, and the eyes and the mouth have a high percentage of these muscles. The baby seems to be programmed to focus on the face—that is, the use of facial expressions as a signaling system between baby and caregiver appears to be part of our biological programming (Basch, 1976, 1988; Stern, 1985). The affect of interest is used by the baby as a way to gather information.

How do somewhat older babies show interest? They play with mobiles in their cribs; they play with their fingers and toes, exploring their bodies; they play with noises, gurgling and cooing; they play with their caregivers through touch, vocalizations, and facial expressions. These are all manifestations of the interest affect. And these babies are learning about their environment and themselves.

As infants get a bit older, their interest affect may be expressed in slightly more sophisticated ways. They will pick up things, examine them with their hands, put them in their mouths, crawl toward them, and listen intently to them. They will use all their senses: touch, taste, sight, hearing, smell.

Infant observation research and clinical work with babies and young children demonstrate how pervasive and intense the expression of interest can be. These exploratory, searching activities are crucial to children's learning about themselves and their world. But interest does not only involve children's learning and exploratory and adapting behaviors . . . it is also responsible for much of their sense of self, identity, and self-esteem. Thus, through their interest, children are not only learning about the world, but they are learning about themselves—what they like, dislike, are good or not so good at doing, and where their passions lie.

The child's self and self-esteem involve complex interactions between what she brings into the world (in self-psychological terms, the *nuclear self* and *independent center of initiative*) and how the environment (*caregivers, traumas*, etc.) treats her. Nature and nurture. Or, as Donald Winnicott terms them in the title of his book *The Maturational Processes and the Facilitating Environment* (1965a).

The interest affect has special importance in this process of establishment of a child's sense of self: It involves his passions, talents, and later ideals and values. Tomkins again: "It is interest . . . which is primary . . . [Interest] supports both what is necessary for life and what is possible" (1962, pp. 343, 345). Finding what we are interested in can help overcome major traumas and the destructive power of negative affects. Negative affects such as fear and shame can wreak havoc with the interest affect and developing self.

Understanding, Sharing, and Validating a Child's Interests

Hopefully, the goals of parents and caregivers or teachers include eliciting who the child is—what the *child's* interests are. This process involves the developmental capacities of the caregivers to see the child as a separate individual, with his own personality and interests—to be able to be empathic with the child, that is, achieve self-and-object differentiation . . . to *elicit* from the child, rather than impose on the child. Or to use self-psychological terms—to follow the nuclear program of the child's self, the independent center of initiative (Kohut, 1977), rather than robbing the child of his volition (Gedo, 2005).

The infant researcher Daniel Stern (1985) has described the importance of these validating processes on the part of the parents. His concept of affect attunement involves understanding and sharing the baby's feelings and conveying that back to the baby. How do we convey this with respect to the feeling of interest, what the baby is intrigued with?

One technique used to address these issues is called "floortime," developed by Stanley Greenspan (1992), a psychiatrist and child-development researcher. Floortime was initially used by clinicians to help assess infants and young children with problems. It turns out that floortime is a marvelous way for parents to better understand their children and enhance the parent-child relationship. The idea is to get down on the floor with babies or young children for 10 or 15 minutes and play whatever and however they want to play. Then follow their lead, be the gracious assistant, let them do what they want to do, do as they ask, and let them lead the way.

Several important processes are occurring here.

- There is interest in the child per se, interest in the child for him- or herself.
- The child is experiencing that her *affect* of interest itself is important. There is interest in and validation of the process of the child's affect of interest and its

Photo 4.2 Stanley Greenspan
Source: Marty Katz/washingtonphotographer.com

importance. This provides support and value for the child's own curiosity, which will enhance learning and self-reflection.
- There is interest in the *content* of the child's ideas and validation of those ideas. The child is getting a sense that her interests and feelings are being understood, validated, and responded to. This helps her understand herself better, aids her reality processing, and gives her the relationship-enhancing experience of the caregiver being interested in her and what intrigues her.
- The caregiver learns about the child—the child shows who she is, what she likes and is interested in, what she can and can't do yet, and where she is developmentally.

In addition, it is helpful to put words to this process: "Oh, you like this, don't you? That was neat what you did, fitting that piece into the other one." Infants and young children understand verbalization and tone of voice much more than may be apparent. As discussed in more detail in Chapters 9 and 10, it is never too early to start putting words to the infant's feelings—labeling the affects (e.g., Katan, 1961; Vivona, 2012, 2014, 2019; Salomonsson, 2006, 2014).

What about the child's environment—the caregivers and their interest in the child? The caregivers may be interested in the child per se, or in the content of the child's interests, or both, or neither. Clinically, these dynamics may be seen in the child's various relationships and even at different times in the same relationship. Awareness of these patterns can be useful in understanding and navigating the child's development.

It is interesting to note that "the gleam in the eye" is not merely a metaphor related to the pleasure and joy that a youngster or parent may experience when feelings of recognition, interest, or validation are elicited. The lachrymal glands are best known for secreting fluid in association with negative affects—tears of distress, rage, and so on. However, as Darwin noted long ago in *The Expression of the Emotions in Man and Animals*, the lachrymal glands of the eye frequently secrete fluid at times of heightened pleasure and excitement, leading to "the gleam in the eye"—"No doubt extreme joy by itself tends to act on the lachrymal glands" (Darwin, 1872b, p. 214).

Enhancing Interest: Bret, *Green Eggs and Ham*, Carl

Bret

An example of children's curiosity and learning may be fun. Years ago, I was visiting my friend Roger, his wife Sally, and their one-and-a-half-year-old son, Bret. Bret was eating in his highchair, and at one point, he slowly picked up a pea and dropped it on the floor. Then he did this with a second pea . . . and a third. I was entranced . . . and so was he, riveted as the pea fell to the floor. He seemed to like peas, as he was eating them as well. I took a pea and joined him . . . I dropped it on the floor! He was intrigued. I had read Alison Gopnik's work (e.g., *The Scientist in the Crib*, 1999) on children's learning and hypothesis-testing. Was he checking out gravity? Would the peas bounce like a ball? Was he bored or just trying to get some interaction with his parents or me? So . . . I got into a little trouble with Roger and Sally, which was followed by interesting discussions . . . Was I encouraging malfeasance and messiness? Or were Bret and I engaged in scientific explorations? Or both? The issues involved in this vignette regarding curiosity and learning will be continued in Chapter 8 as we explore cognition and development.

Green Eggs and Ham

Illustrations of transformations of affects are found throughout this book. Those transformations that result in interest and curiosity are especially significant because interest and curiosity enhance empathy. A unique example is found in children's literature, namely, the Dr. Seuss book *Green Eggs and Ham* (Geisel, 1960). Recall that one character is convinced that he doesn't like green eggs and ham. The other character—Sam-I-Am—strives to get him to try green eggs and ham. Finally, the first character does try them . . . and likes them! As the psychoanalyst Michael Basch noted, the book conveys the affective transformation from disgust to interest (personal communication). I would add that the affective transformation also includes the shift from other negative affects—e.g., distress, anger, fear, shame—to interest and enjoyment.

Carl

I have a friend, Carl, about 50 years old, whose house was invaded by "stink bugs," a large insect that exudes a malodorous smell, especially when threatened or crushed. The odor permeates upholstery, clothing, and fabric . . . and lingers.

He reported that these creatures are attracted to light, crawl into anything, and are noisy when flying, making it hard to fall or stay asleep. He was reluctant to use pesticide in the house since it is not very effective, and when the bugs die, they stain the house with their odor, attracting other insects and mice. Feeling beset and helpless, he found he was constantly agitated by them. It became a one-on-one war of wills with the invaders. He called them "the enemy."

So he started to research them and see what solutions were available. He learned that their scientific name is *Halyomorpha halys*, and that their back forms a heraldic-shield shape veined like marble. He learned that the bugs don't sting or bite. They can walk on surfaces upside-down; squeeze through very small spaces; and when outside, they fly remarkably fast. The trick is to keep them out of the house by blocking openings, even rubbing screens with odorous sheets to repel them. He set to work to make his house a fortress!

But as he was trying to beat them back, he was also learning more and more about their remarkable abilities and found he was intrigued. He reported that the more he understood about the insects, the less fearful he became. Eventually, he felt his curiosity and interest were replacing his anxiety. True, he removed them from the house and kept them from reentering. But he reported to me that the main thing he learned was that he could replace fear and anger if he stimulated his curiosity and interest. In a sense, he was describing a desensitization process—increasing his interest and decreasing negative affects (distress, fear, disgust) of a stimulus (stink bug) that had previously caused such feelings.

In summary, I have been discussing the importance of interest and transformations of negative affects to positive, i.e., interest and enjoyment. The next section deals with the interference of interest.

Interfering With Interest

Here, I will try to illustrate with everyday examples a few ways in which interest can be impaired. Much of what I see clinically involves interference with and inhibition of interest. Any excessive negative affects can interfere with interest: distress, anger, fear, shame, disgust, and dissmell. Fear and shame are most toxic to interest: Fear often results in repression and shame in disavowal (Basch, 1983b, 1988). For example, consider selective mutism, seen in children who have stopped talking, usually outside the home. Clinically, this process is often rooted in fear of expressing affects, especially anger (e.g., Yanof, 1996; Holinger, 2016).

Also at issue here is the question of learning. With the impairment of curiosity, the sense of self and self-esteem may be threatened: To consider new information and ways of thinking may be disruptive (see Chapters 7 and 13). Another aspect of learning and inhibition of interest resides in the educational systems themselves. Specifically, the question arises about enlarging the time in school for children and adolescents to pursue their own passions rather than having to spend so much time on topics and courses deemed to be essential by education groups and teachers.

Interest can be inhibited throughout development. An anxious mother, reacting to the intense eye-to-eye gaze of her breast-feeding baby, may use fear, shame, or anger to get the baby to disconnect and turn away. As the infant becomes more mobile, the interferences with interest are even more apparent. These patterns of responding or not responding to the baby may be passed down and repeated from one generation to the next, becoming intergenerational (e.g., Goodfriend, 1993). A depressed mother whose own cries were not heard may repeat this with her own children. This situation forms the basis for one of the best-known articles in the infant/child literature, "Ghosts in the Nursery," by Selma Fraiberg and her colleagues (1975).

A child's curiosity and safety often create dilemmas. Virginia Demos (1994) gives a nice example. Suppose the infant spots a pair of scissors and crawls toward them. As the infant reaches for them, the caregiver yells, "No! Stop!" But, asks Demos, stop what? Stop being interested in scissors? Stop being interested in new objects? Stop exploring? The caregiver has acted to help prevent possible harm to the baby but has not validated the interest affect, helped them safely explore scissors, or shifted the interest to a safer object. The command is simply no. Instead, when the child is safe, the caregiver might embrace the curiosity and also explain the potential dangers.

Parents often use fear and anger to interfere with a toddler's explorations, especially where safety is involved. "No! Don't touch that wire!" "Look out—don't go into the street!" The parents' anger is understandable. Any excessive negative affect—in this case, the parent's fear—can be "too much" and become expressed as anger. The parent's anger is then transmitted to the child along with the fear. Using words to discuss the danger and appreciate the curiosity can be useful.

Speaking of fear, recall the old adage: "Curiosity killed the cat." This certainly conveys the inhibition of interest. There exists another proverb related to this issue: "Cats have nine lives." So again, we have the tension between interest and fear, positive and negative affects. These dynamics are discussed further in Chapter 13 on bias and prejudice.

I recall an episode when our son was young, and we invited a few of his friends and their parents, whom we did not really know, over for a playdate. The children were all having fun, running around, getting into things, and so on. But one father became increasingly anxious about his son's behavior (which was not out of the ordinary). "Don't touch that, Jim . . . don't go over there . . . no running . . ." etc. His son started slowing down, becoming less and less active and happy. Finally, his father said, "Jim, if you do that one more time, I'm going to have to get my belt out . . ." Jim became almost immobile and mute the rest of the afternoon. The distress, fear, and shame were palpable. The use of the negative affects had shut down the curiosity and playing and creating. I never did figure out what was triggering his father's anxiety.

Parents also often use disgust to interfere with a child's interest. For example, a little girl has some candy gummy worms, and instead of eating them, she has become intrigued with touching and mashing them. She begins to squeeze them through her fingers. She keeps doing this, and the gummy worms turn into a multicolored paste and fragments. Mother sees this, makes a face, and says, "Oooohh, yuck, disgusting!" The child may react by stopping her play with the gummy worms.

The infant and small child may have varied reactions to the interruption or interference with interest. If she is playing with a small car that is then taken away, she may get angry. If the child is playing with a wire and suddenly the mother yells and swoops down to take him away, he may show fear. If a child happens to look intensely at a person who turns out to be a stranger, the child may be told it is impolite to stare, eliciting shame in response to her interest.

How might interest be inhibited in the verbal child? Recall the idea of "minimize affect inhibition." This applies to verbal expression as well. Thus, if a child is angry and says, "I hate you," he is often met with pushback rather than exploration and discussion: "Don't talk to me that way" or "We don't use those words here." Anger is frequently seen clinically in the therapeutic relationship and negative transference, and it is essential to accept it and sort out what underlies it, not suppress it. Similarly, in development, parents have an opportunity to explore what the child is distressed and angry about. Other common reactions that may interfere with the interest of the verbal child include: "Mind your own business;" "Why are you always asking 'why'?" "Shut up!" "Because I said so."

In short, the affect of interest is crucial to human beings, and it is often underestimated. I turn now to processes that are intimately connected with interest—playing and creating—and explore the affects that appear to underlie these important functions. Affect theory may provide a more comprehensive explanation of the dynamics of playing and creating.

Chapter 5

Affects
The Foundation of Playing and Creating

Chapter Outline:

- Playing, creating, and affects
- Playing and creating in action
- Inhibition and impairment of playing and creating
- Playing and creating as a developmental process: Transitional objects and pets
- Playing and creating and clinical issues

In Donald Winnicott's seminal book *Playing and Reality*, he stresses that only in play can we find ourselves:

> It is in playing and only in playing that the individual child or adult is able to be creative and to use the whole personality, and it is only in being creative that the individual discovers the self.
>
> (1971, p. 54)

Playing and creating are important aspects of human development as well as clinical treatment. They power much of our capacity to learn, explore, establish a sense of self, and understand ourselves and our interests. There is a great deal of technical and popular literature on playing and creating; I want to discuss them somewhat differently—namely, through the perspective of their underlying affects and their roles in development and clinical work.

Playing, Creating, and Affects

Playing and creating combine elements of various affects, especially interest, enjoyment, and surprise. In addition, the affects of distress, anger, fear, and shame may impair play and creativity. By considering playing and creating through the lens of affects, there is an opportunity to augment those life-enhancing activities and help prevent their disruption.

Playing, then, can be defined as the interaction of the affects of interest, enjoyment, and surprise. Or, to put it differently, the interaction of the affects of interest, enjoyment, and surprise may produce what we call *playing*. *Creating* is an extension—or cousin—of playing, containing new, innovative, imaginative elements. This combination of playing and creating can have a great impact on the other two information processing systems we are considering, namely, cognition and language.

Playing and Creating in Action

So, let's look at playing and creating through the lens of positive and negative affects and see how affects enhance or inhibit a child's (and an adult's) playing and creating. Tomkins links play with interest and discusses maximizing play:

> *The child is encouraged and permitted to play with parents, with peers, and by himself. Many interactions are converted into games and playful rituals which otherwise might be neutral, dull or unpleasant. Play is regarded as an end in itself.*
>
> (Demos, 1995, p. 170, emphasis added)

Playing and creating appear when they are fueled by the affects of interest, enjoyment, and surprise. The process also seems to involve alternating between surprise, interest, and enjoyment. Surprise can quickly become tinged with positive or negative affects. Even if a negative affect is briefly elicited (e.g., fear or distress), a reduction of stimuli (enjoyment) can be experienced as pleasurable, as in play.

Here's an example of the role of positive affects in playing. Some years ago, I was bouncing a ball back and forth with a little girl who was about one-and-a-half or two years old. As described in Chapter 3, it was stunning to see the affective expressions flicker rapidly across her face. Recall that affective responses to stimuli can occur in milliseconds and then be sustained or changed. The affects of surprise, interest, and enjoyment were oscillating as we bounced the ball back and forth between us. The way her affects were interacting in our ball game made up her "playing."

Playing and creating are apparent from infancy through old age. Babies may use their eyes and noises from their mouths to play with mom and dad and themselves (Stern, 1985). Young children may use blocks to build structures and towns, clothes to play dress up, toy trucks to build roads, and footstools to ride horses. These enterprises may have a variety of meanings. Playing and creating in older children, adolescents, and adults are seen in various activities: art, sports, writing, music, relationships, and psychological treatment. They are also seen in science. For example, Charles Darwin's manner when he worked in his 60s was described by his son Francis as bright and animated—play-like!

> His love of each particular experiment, and his eager zeal not to lose the fruit of it came out markedly in these crossing experiments—in the elaborate care he took not to make any confusion in putting capsules in the wrong trays, &c. &c. I can recall his appearance as he counted seeds under the simple microscope

with an alertness not usually characterizing such mechanical work as counting. I think he personified each seed as a small demon trying to elude him by getting into the wrong heap or jumping away altogether, and this gave to the work the excitement of a game.

(Browne, 2002, pp. 414–415)

Inhibition and Impairment of Playing and Creating

Both playing and creating can be profoundly inhibited by eliciting negative affects such as distress, anger, fear, and shame. I mentioned the poignant example of Jim in Chapter 4. Negative affects can curtail the child's interest and enjoyment, which fuels playing. Negative affects can also hamper the capacity to think expansively, for example, in the process of creating. All this highlights the remarkable impact parents and caregivers can have on development, both positive and negative. Heinz Kohut described these processes with his ideas of the importance of psychological oxygen throughout development and treatment—selfobject functioning, provision of an enhancing environment, validation, empathy, and so on (1971, 1977, 1984; Modell, 1976; Newman, 1999; Galatzer-Levy & Cohler, 1993).

Playing and Creating as a Developmental Process: Transitional Objects and Pets

I am especially interested in the role of affects in understanding playing and creating in development. Donald Winnicott (1953, 1971) and Stanley Greenspan (1992, 1997) are among those whose ideas are intriguing.

For example, Winnicott asks us to consider transitional objects—the child's teddy bear, blanket, lovey, whatever. The term *transitional* refers roughly to the arena between the internal world of the child and the external world. These transitional objects can provide a variety of functions: companionship, comfort, love, consolation, tension-regulation, play, a target for love and anger, and the like. The child imparts a variety of affects, motives, and actions to the object.

Pets provide similar functions for both children and adults. It is difficult to overestimate the importance of transitional objects and pets for human beings. I have begun to consider pets as what I call "living transitional objects." Jennifer Lock Oman wrote a nationally distributed column for the *Des Moines Register/Gannett News Syndicate* for over ten years. She stated that the column that generated the most response by far involved the death of a pet and the grieving process afterward (personal communication).

My son's primary transitional object was a stuffed animal . . . a small black-and-white-spotted dog he named Pinto. When he was about four years old, I was watching him playing vigorously with Pinto, and I said something like: "Pinto really is a remarkable dog, isn't he? You and he can play together, and he comforts you and you comfort him, and he loves you and you love him, and you can also get mad at him and he at you, but then you can both love each

Photo 5.1 Donald Winnicott
Source: By permission of The Marsh Agency Ltd., on behalf of The Winnicott Trust CIO 1174533

other again . . ." and so on. He turned to me and said: "Daddy, how do you know all that?!" I was stunned . . . I think I responded that Donald Winnicott had helped me.

Winnicott expanded his concept into what he termed *transitional phenomena* and *transitional space*:

> We experience life in the area of transitional phenomena, in the exciting interweave of subjectivity and objective observation, and in an area that is intermediate between the inner reality of the individual and the shared reality of the world that is external to individuals.
>
> (1971, p. 64)

He noted that playing and creating are related to transitional phenomena and can be conceptualized as a way of reaching authentic, creative, less-defended parts of a person's personality—i.e., the True Self, in terms of his True and False Self distinction (1960).

Winnicott suggested that it is creative self-awareness

> more than anything else that makes the individual feel that life is worth living. Contrasted with this is a relationship to external reality which is one of compliance, the world and its details being recognized but only as something to be fitted in with or demanding adaptation.
>
> (1971, p. 65)

Winnicott discussed this in his paper "Ego Distortion in Terms of True and False Self" (1960), and others have explored it as well (e.g., Alice Miller's *The Drama of the Gifted Child*, 2008/1979). I am considering here the synergistic interplay between subjective and objective, internal and external, the child's inner self and compliance with the external environment.

Daniel Stern was particularly gifted in describing the internal-external interactions in the early development of the self—the first one-and-a-half years—as he discussed in *The Interpersonal World of the Infant* (1985). Stanley Greenspan also draws attention to the role of affects, playing, and creating in development. As described in Chapter 4, Greenspan conceived of "floortime" to focus on eliciting the internal interests of the child rather than imposing from the external environment.

Playing and Creating and Clinical Issues

In the face of various feelings of vulnerability, anxiety, and helplessness, young children will often play games in which they take on the role of superheroines or superheroes, princesses or princes, cowgirls or cowboys, etc. Fantasy and games are among the ways children regulate tension, deal with trauma, and experiment with the real world.

One example involves Sigmund Freud and his description of his one-and-a-half-year-old grandson's game "fort-da" ("gone-there"), which emerged during short separations from his mother (1920). One day, his mother was gone briefly . . .

> The child had a wooden reel with a piece of string tied around it . . . What he did was to hold the reel by the string and very skilfully [sic] throw it over the edge of his curtained cot, so that it disappeared into it, at the same time uttering his expressive "0-0-0-0" ("fort"—gone). He then pulled the reel out of the cot again by the string and hailed its reappearance with a joyful "*da*" ("there"). This, then was the complete game—disappearance and return.
>
> (p. 15)

Another example comes to mind from an occasion when my two-year-old son was playing alone in the front seat of the family car. The car was resting on a slightly declining driveway with the engine off, the gear in "park," and the key out. Somehow, he jiggled the gear into neutral, and the car slowly went down the driveway and crashed gently against some bushes and a fence. My son, unhurt, slowly emerged from the car and ran to me in the garage. For weeks afterward, he took his little construction toys down to the place where the car had crashed and spent hours digging and constructing in that area.

A final example involves a girl who was four years old and living in New York when the planes crashed into the Twin Towers on 9/11. Over the next many days, she and her family talked about and watched what had happened. During this time, the child took out her blocks, built tall buildings, and took a toy plane and crashed it into the buildings, toppling them.

Playing is one of the major techniques in all child therapy, beginning with Hermine Hug-Hellmuth, Melanie Klein, Anna Freud, and others (Geissman & Geissman, 1998). Through their play, children express their feelings, thoughts, and ideas, thus helping therapists to understand them, even if the children cannot discuss them. It is the task of the therapist to begin to carve out meanings and feelings from the playful and creative behaviors and actions. This ultimately leads to enhanced verbalization of affects (see Chapter 11). This process can also be seen in work with mothers and infants (Winnicott, 1971; Fraiberg et al., 1975; Stern, 1985; Salomonsson, 2006, 2014, 2016).

Often, however, the journey toward understanding, verbalizing, and discussing feelings, actions, and motivations is a long and arduous one. Play and action rule the day. As a six-year-old patient once said to me, putting his hand out: "Talk to the hand, not to the head!" and "Let's just play, Doc!"

Photo 5.2 Melanie Klein

Source: Douglas Glass, CC BY 4.0 <https://creativecommons.org/licenses/by/4.0>, via Wikimedia Commons

Photo 5.3 Anna Freud
Source: © Freud Museum London

There has emerged a large literature dealing with the technical issues involving play and child analysis and therapy (e.g., Winnicott, 1971; Weiss, 1981; Valeros, 1989; Yanof, 1996, 2019; Hurry, 1998; Holinger, 2016). To oversimplify to some extent, clinical treatment of both children and adults seems to involve two major processes:

1 Verbal interpretations—feelings (conscious and unconscious), childhood antecedents, actions, goals, themes, transferences, and so on.
2 The evolving nature of the relationship with the therapist—the interest and empathy of the therapist, the patient's reactions to the therapist, the therapist's reactions to the patient, the internalization of the therapist's capacities for tension-regulation, self-reflection, understanding, and more.

Playing and creating play a major role in both these processes in child and adult therapy. Thus, one of the most fascinating questions emerging in psychotherapy and psychoanalysis involves the mutative aspects of verbal interpretations (e.g., childhood antecedents, transferences, etc.) on the one hand and the therapist-patient relationship and playing on the other (Valeros, 1989). To be sure, this may draw the distinction too starkly, and there is certainly much overlap. However, there are many situations in which playing and the relationship seem to be creating an intrapsychic structure, with rather minimal verbalization. Jose Valeros discusses these issues in a fascinating article—"Coercion: Technical Problems in the Psychoanalysis of Children" (1989). Valeros, in his work with children, suggests that the process of playing often takes center stage in therapeutic change, and efforts to interpret verbally may impede the progress of change. These ideas also appear related to an emerging focus on the mutative aspects of what some have termed "the real relationship" in therapy (e.g., Beiser, 1995).

The changes that take place via playing and the therapeutic relationship can be conceptualized as being associated with affect. During the course of treatment and the relationship, the patient consciously and unconsciously identifies with and internalizes the therapist's capacities for introspection, interest, curiosity, tension-regulation, dealing with ambivalence, and so on—all various aspects of specific affects.

Playing and creating are also important in clinical work with adults, particularly the therapist's capacity to understand and relate to individual patients (e.g., Cooper, 2023). The notion of playing and creating in adult therapy is also associated with the so-called relational and intersubjectivity schools of psychoanalytic thought, with respect to the psychodynamics and mutative influence of the patient-therapist relationship (Winnicott, 1971; Newman, 1999; Jacobs, 1991; Beiser, 1995).

One is indebted to Donald Winnicott for so many insights about playing and creating in development and treatment. He famously noted:

Psychotherapy takes place in the overlap of the two areas of playing, that of the patient and that of the therapist. Psychotherapy has to do with two people playing together . . . where playing is not possible then the work done by the therapist is directed towards bringing the patient from a state of not being able to play into a state of being able to play.

(1971, p. 38, emphasis in original)

I now turn from an exploration of affects in playing and creating to another aspect of development: the role of affects in the need for human beings to be recognized and remembered in their progress toward their sense of self as an independent center of initiative.

Chapter 6

Affects, Early Development, and the Sense of Self

Chapter Outline:

- Affects and early interactions
- Being recognized and remembered
- Throughout development: External support and internal fragility
- Affects and the self in clinical settings

How do people turn out the way they do? Does their sense of self change significantly throughout their lifetime, or is it relatively stable? How resilient and adaptive are human beings in the face of the vagaries of life? How do individuals even begin to describe their sense of self?

The focus in this chapter is on the impact of positive and negative affects on our sense of self. Definitions abound regarding the sense of self, with much important work emerging from the self-psychology theorists and clinicians. For example, Heinz Kohut refers to the self as the independent center of initiative (1977). Arnold Goldberg suggests clarifying the sense of self by considering the brain, mind, and self: One is a vital organ composed of neurons and synapses; one gives meaning and coherence to the internal and external world; and one is the seat of agency (2015).

Throughout this discussion of the self, Tomkins's principles of maximizing positive affects and minimizing negative affects are clearly visible. For instance, David Terman's significant paper "The Negative Selfobject" explicitly highlights the developmental and clinical problems associated with negative affects (2021).

Nature (genetics, etc.), nurture (personal environment, caregiving), and fate—and the interactions of the three—play roles in the construction of our sense of self and personality development. The role and influence of nature, nurture, and fate have engaged philosophers and those interested in psychology for eons. Over the past several decades, there has been much progress in understanding and treating children and adults suffering from what may be called problems in the development of a positive sense of self: profound depression, anxiety and fear, trauma, self-disorders, and other emotional issues.

I am interested in origins and outcomes, and in the innate and environmental variables that affect development. Studying outcomes is very difficult due in large

DOI: 10.4324/9780429203640-7

Photo 6.1 René Spitz
Source: Courtesy of the Denver Institute for Psychoanalysis

part to the number of variables involved. However, it is also important to make the effort for at least two reasons: The first is to understand better how to treat people with various problems. The second reason is perhaps even more important—and that involves efforts at preventing the problems in the first place (e.g., see Chapter 12; Holinger, 2020).

To highlight some of these issues, this chapter looks at the role of affects in early life as related to a sense of self. There's an examination of how the positive affects of interest and enjoyment support early development and the acquisition of an enhanced sense of self, even to the point of the infant's survival. The interest of parents and caregivers seems to give infants what they need in order to feel they exist, are worthy, and are recognized and remembered.

In addition, problematic senses of self will be explored, for example, extreme emotional fragility, excessive need for external praise and validation, and intense longings to be recognized and remembered. This is not meant to be an exhaustive review but rather a discussion of the potential importance of affects in early and subsequent development.

Affects and Early Interactions

Affective interactions are crucial to the development of infants and young children. I will start with René Spitz. In the middle of the 20th century, Spitz studied infants in various institutions. He showed that even if infants were given food, water, clean surroundings, and so on, they often deteriorated and sometimes died if they did not have enough human interaction (1945, 1965). Spitz's findings, termed *hospitalism*, made it necessary to take into account the emotional needs of babies admitted to institutions. These studies helped make it possible for parents to stay with their children when they were admitted to a hospital. Over the decades, many others have followed in Spitz's footsteps with both clinical and theoretical advances and have shown various aspects of the importance of early interactions with infants (e.g., Winnicott, 1958; Fraiberg et al., 1975; Fraiberg, 1980; Goodfriend, 1993; Salomonsson, 2014).

Daniel Stern (1985) and others have described the very early, active affective interaction between infants and caregivers via facial expressions, movements, and voice. The eyes and mouth, with many small muscles, can readily transmit the various affects—interest, joy, surprise, distress, fear, anger, and so on. Stern highlighted how infants relate socially and have various senses of self long before they have self-awareness and language. "Those include the senses of agency, of physical cohesion, of continuity in time, of having intentions in mind and other such experiences" (1985, p. 6). Stern examined these processes in detail in his elaboration of four senses of self: emergent, core, subjective, and verbal.

Virginia Demos (2019) noted that these interactions and other data from infant studies have led several to suggest an attachment drive (e.g., Bowlby, 1969; Sroufe & Waters, 1977; Ainsworth et al., 1978). In contrast, Demos and others suggest that attachment theory represents a higher-level construct (1989, 2019), with *affects* underlying aspects of attachment and with the quality of attachment being mediated by affects.

These early relational issues have been addressed by many individuals and theoretical models (e.g., Greenberg & Mitchell, 1983; Bacal & Newman, 1990). For example, child analysis and self-psychology are well-known for both their clinical recommendations and descriptions of the feeling states in early problematic relationships, including fragmentation and nonexistence. As Adam Phillips notes about Winnicott's ideas, "Not to be seen by the mother, at least at the moment of the spontaneous gesture, is not to exist" (1988, p. 130).

I suggest that understanding the innate affects and how they function enhances an appreciation of what helps and hinders development in a child's early years. On the one hand, children benefit from an emphasis on the positive affects of interest and enjoyment (e.g., Tomkins, 1963). On the other hand, excessive use of the negative affects of fear, shame, distress, and anger are more likely to result in problems (Terman, 2021).

Characterological patterns can be readily and often unconsciously transferred from one generation to the next. So even if a parent agrees that interacting and motivating via positive affects are generally beneficial for a child, it may be difficult for that parent to change lifelong, generational habits of behavior. This is one reason why the parent's work in child therapy is so important (Novick & Novick, 2005).

The affects of interest and enjoyment seem to be crucial for early development and the sense of self. But then questions arise—interest in what? Parents can be interested in their baby, or in their baby's interests, or in their baby's affect of interest itself . . . or all of these, none of these, or any combination of those. Stanley

Affects, Early Development, and the Sense of Self 57

Greenspan's writings on early interactions with the baby (1992, 1997—"floortime") can be seen as highlighting the affects of interest and enjoyment and *eliciting from* the child—rather than *imposing on*—likes and dislikes. All of this is a step toward self-reflection, self-understanding, and a more solid sense of self.

Being Recognized and Remembered

Humans need emotional interaction and external support both early on and throughout their lifespan. Some seem to need it less than others. Some seem to need it more. John Adams, the second president of the United States, noted the "passion for distinction" in men and women: "Whether they be old or young, rich or poor, high or low, wise or foolish, ignorant or learned, every individual is seen to be strongly actuated by a desire to be seen, heard, talked of, approved and respected" (McCullough, 2002, p. 421). Manifestations of the need for external reinforcement for the internal world can be seen in everyday life as well as in politics, science, art, and play.

The intensity of the need to be remembered, to leave a legacy, appears commonplace. Yet, there seems to be a disconnect here. Geologic time shows our universe to be about 13.77 billion years old, our solar system about 4.57 billion years old, and our Earth about 4.54 billion years old. In 100 to 200 years from now, how many people will be readily remembered from the 21st century? How about 500 years from now . . . maybe 10 to 20, perhaps more by historians and specialists in various fields? How about 10,000 years from now? 100,000 years?

Evolutionary paleontologists such as Darwin (1859), Stephen Jay Gould (1993), Ernst Mayr (2001), and others note that more than 99 percent of all species that ever lived on Earth are now extinct. The contradiction between the need to be remembered and the element of time would suggest a cognitive deficit in reality-processing (*denial* or *disavowal*) (Basch, 1983b; Gedo, 2005). Perhaps this is needed to fend off fear of death, feelings of nonexistence, loss of stimulation, aloneness, and separation. With regard to these types of feelings, Steven Weinberg,

Photo 6.2 Stephen Jay Gould

Nobel laureate in physics, famously wrote in *The First Three Minutes*: "The more the universe seems comprehensible, the more it also seems pointless." Yet he followed it up with this sentence: "But if there is no solace in the fruits of our research, there is at least some consolation in the research itself" (1977, p. 154). Again, the negative affects of distress and fear are counteracted by interest (curiosity) and enjoyment.

The issue of religion also comes into play here. Some discuss religion in terms of an illusion, as Freud did in *The Future of an Illusion* (1927)—an externalization of an internal wish for an all-powerful caregiver to alleviate some of the distress, fears, and unpredictability surrounding life and death. Others, for instance, Kohut, focus on the benefits of religion from an empathic perspective, enhancing life through the decrease of tension, creating a sense of being of value and of belonging, bringing meaning and psychological coherence into our lives (Strozier et al., 2022; see also Chapter 13). Winnicott describes similar functions provided by early-in-life "transitional objects," the relationship between the child and a favorite blanket, "lovey," pets, and so on—that is, a loving, soothing, encouraging presence that stabilizes the sense of self and helps the child feel recognized, acknowledged, and of value (1953).

Throughout Development: External Support and Internal Fragility

What is the effect on children who do not get the early positive responses and affective interaction they need? The outcome depends on many variables, ranging from that child's innate character to the support of ancillary environmental factors and people. As a result, infants who don't get early positive responses and affirmative interaction may grow into children, adolescents, and adults with no problems, or they may contend with depression, anxiety, and so on.

Here, I am looking at how personality development may be distorted through neglect of positive affects as well as excessive negative affects and lead to children and adults who need excessive praise, validation, recognition, and remembrance. As Terman noted:

> The powerful shaping function of caretaker responses can often shape the emergent self as bad, worthless, depleted and defective. These inner shapes of the self are derived from interactions with caretakers in which the affect of the caretaker include rage, censure, indifference. They occur in the context of the child's need for affirmation and response.
>
> (2021, p. 380)

These people may present in many ways: sad, depressed, angry, clingy, hungry for attention, "look at me"; bombastic, grandiose, full of themselves (*compensatory grandiosity*), and calling for praise. It is not difficult to see the intrinsic deficit—the lack of a solid sense of self, a lack of self-cohesion, an intense need to be recognized and remembered. What they seem to want is encouragement, praise, psychological oxygen, validation, and so on from extrinsic sources to shore up their intrinsic vulnerability.

It is these types of narcissistic vulnerabilities that Heinz Kohut and his colleagues addressed systematically as disorders of the self (1971, 1977, 1984). Tom Kohut, Heinz Kohut's son, is a historian who has written a wonderful essay on Kaiser Wilhelm II of Germany (1859–1941) and his narcissistic or "self-pathology" (2011). T. Kohut vividly describes Wilhelm's brittle self-certainty and fragile sense of self-esteem, extreme vulnerability, and rage when insufficiently appreciated, and his grandiosity and craving for external reassurance, admiration, and appreciation.

External validation and support may be transformative throughout the life cycle. In the following vignette, the singer Jewel describes the impact Bob Dylan had on her during their interactions in the 1990s.

> The thing that was most important to me was that he really believed in me. He liked my art, and nobody did at the time. The press was calling me a mistake, a Pollyanna, naïve, dumb. My music wasn't going anywhere. And the fact that Dylan liked me . . . I remember thinking, *Well, if no one else does, that's fine!* It was very validating and very rewarding to have someone you think of as a hero ask, "Why did you write this lyric? What were you thinking about during this lyric? What are you reading right now?" He'd give me books to read, music to listen to. He liked that I was solo acoustic. He was like, "Just keep going." It definitely invigorated me.
> (Pelly, 2021, emphasis in original)

Dylan's personal interactions with Jewel, and her idealization of him, are a nice example of the potential impact of positive affects—interest and validation—provision of selfobject functions and the development of the self.

Another poignant example of this issue of external validation and connection involves Heinz Kohut himself and his father, who was a musician and artistically inclined. As an adolescent, Heinz became increasingly interested in medical issues. Kohut said:

> In reality, these questions reflected my own interests . . . I kept asking these kind of questions . . . He became visibly annoyed with me and said, "Why are you interested in such questions? Why can't you be like other boys?" I remember being very hurt. I had the feeling that there was some kind of gap—some kind of distance that existed between my father and me—that there was something in me that I was deeply interested in which annoyed him . . . Well, it was a long, long hard road from that time on . . . But then came the time when I was a late adolescent and I got into medical school and I wrote several scientific papers and he was very impressed by my work. One day he said to me, "You know, Heinz, you have done things that I could never do. I'm *very* proud of you." I was extremely pleased by this, as you can imagine.
> (Kohut, 1994, p. 373, italics in original)

Affects and the Self in Clinical Settings

Clinically, people who seem to be quite fragile internally and who often need extensive external validation to maintain a more solid sense of themselves have been given various diagnoses, including borderline, narcissistic character disorders, and self-disorders. Extreme manifestations of these needs may be related to schizophrenia or bipolar disorders.

Child analysis, relational studies, and infant research have made well-known contributions to the understanding of this self-fragility (Geissman & Geissman, 1998; Greenberg & Mitchell, 1983; Stern, 1985). For example, Adler and Buie (1979) suggested early relationship disruptions could later make it difficult to hold the therapist (and others) in their minds and internalize their functions, hence the need for external support. There are many clinical theories and techniques that have emerged over the years that seek to understand and deal with these problems. For instance, Fred Pine's work *Drive, Ego, Object, & Self: A Synthesis for Clinical Work* highlights four major psychoanalytic perspectives (1990). The importance of affects in all these is noteworthy.

With respect to the problems of the self as focused on in this chapter, Winnicott, Kohut, Kernberg, Modell, and many others have enhanced the understanding of the nature of early disturbances and important clinical interventions. Winnicott (1958, 1965b) and Kohut (1971, 1977) were especially influential in understanding and detoxifying narcissistic issues and their origins, as well as enhancing therapeutic options. Kohut, in particular, focused on understanding and treating adults with narcissistic problems, more recently termed *self-disorders* (1971, 1977, 1984).

Photo 6.3 Heinz Kohut
Source: Courtesy of Tom Kohut

While it is beyond my scope to discuss this work in detail, a brief description conveys the use of affect in the clinical process. Kohut and Wolfe noted that

> If the analyst can show to the patient who demands praise that, despite the availability of average external responses, he must continue to "fish for compliments" because the hopeless need of the unmirrored child in him remains unassuaged, and if he can show to the raging patient the helplessness and hopelessness that lie behind his rages, can show him that indeed his rage is the direct consequence of the fact that he can not assert his demands effectively, then the old needs will slowly begin to make their appearance more openly as the patient becomes more empathic with himself . . . Experience teaches us, in other words, that the therapist's major effort must be concentrated on the task of keeping the old needs mobilized. If he succeeds in this, then they will gradually—and spontaneously—be transformed into normal self-assertiveness and normal devotion to ideals.
> (1978, p. 423)

It is interesting to note that of all our clinical theories and models, self-psychology seems particularly connected with affect theory and Tomkins's work (e.g., Terman, 2021).

As Kohut's work progressed, he explored the connections and differences between self-psychology and drive and other theories, particularly within the context of development, childhood antecedents, and trauma. His thoughts on the integrations of these theoretical conceptualizations in various types of psychopathologies are available in a remarkable series of lectures ("informal talks") he gave at the Chicago Institute for Psychoanalysis from 1972–1976 (Tolpin & Tolpin, 1996). They convey some of Kohut's ideas about the oscillations between fragile and more solid senses of self, particularly as these differences might relate to earlier developmental issues and current environmental challenges (e.g., pp. 259–273). These discussions were recorded, edited, and published. They are available thanks to the work of Paul Tolpin and Marian Tolpin, and they make for fascinating reading.

Understanding the specific affects and their functioning can be useful in this clinical work, both therapeutic and preventive. As noted previously, some separate the mutative functions of psychoanalytic work into two overlapping branches: the relationship with the therapist and interpretation.

- Elements of the relationship consist of aspects of the verbal and action elements between patient and therapist, for example, various internalizations and empathic immersion (e.g., Kohut, 1971), identifications, learning, and the so-called real relationship (Beiser, 1995).
- Interpretive elements could include transference, childhood antecedents, patterns, goals, and so on.

For instance, in working with both relationship and interpretive elements, a focus on innate affects (such as interest, anger, and shame) can enlarge and deepen the understanding of those affective states and antecedents. What was the nature of the lack of interest the patient felt as a child or feels now with the therapist? Interest in what? In their well-being? Their self? Their own interests? Their thoughts, feelings, erotic interests? Or, if a perceived lack of interest . . . why? What is not of interest? And of course, these questions are raised internally by the analyst as well with respect to countertransference issues.

Perhaps most important is exploring the process of patients' interest and curiosity about themselves, the grounds for self-reflection and self-analytic work. All of this can then be used to understand better a patient's possible childhood antecedents: What was the nature of the neglect, deficit, or misunderstandings? Similarly, the various aspects of the patient-therapist relationship can be explored with an eye to specific affects—a reciprocal process of sorting out words, actions, and provision of function between the two people and the specific affects involved (Stern, 1985; Newman, 1999; Holinger, 1999).

With respect to the possibility of minimizing or preventing difficulties of internal vulnerabilities and self-cohesion, how might we best elicit a child's genuine interests and sense of self? In terms of affects, major benefits occur by focusing on the positive affects of interest and enjoyment and minimizing negative affects such as distress, anger, fear, and shame. A classic example of this is the problem of physical and degrading punishment, which is explored in detail later (see Chapter 12).

Chapters 4, 5, and 6 have focused on interest and how positive affects can enhance development. We turn now to an affect that tends not to be overlooked but is often misunderstood—anger. Anger is the final common pathway of negative affects when they become excessive, potentially impairing aspects of development.

Chapter 7

Anger
The Misunderstood Affect

Chapter Outline:

- Anger as an affect
- Anger and fear
- Some clinical and theoretical issues
- A clinical illustration and discussion

Anger as an Affect

Anger seems so often to be misunderstood. Anger, like all affects, is a signal—to others and to oneself. Anger could be termed an SOS signal, a call for help: "Something is wrong here!" As Silvan Tomkins notes, "All the negative affects trouble human beings deeply . . . Anger is problematic above all" (1991, p. 111). Even Aristotle noted in *The Nicomachean Ethics* in 340 BC,

> Anyone can get angry—that is easy . . . but to do this to the right person, to the right extent, at the right time, with the right motive, and in the right way, that is not for everyone, nor is it easy.

As discussed in Chapter 3, anger is one of several innate affects, a response to both internal and external stimulation. Anger is linked to the affect of distress. Everyone has a stimulus threshold that can trigger distress and anger.

With infants and young children, any excessive sustained increase in the level of stimulation, such as a bright light, loud noise, hunger, fatigue, or illness, may activate distress: annoyance, irritability, arched eyebrows, corners of the mouth turned down, tears and crying, and so on. If the stimulation persists and heightens, anger is triggered: frowning eyebrows, narrowed eyes, red face, the roar of rage.

With older children and adults, the stimuli may be quite varied: stress involving school pressures, parental expectations, peers; work, children, spouse; physical pain; conscious and unconscious fantasies; and so on. Distress increases, and annoyance, irritability, and snippiness can morph into anger.

Anger might be termed a quantitative affect: There is "too muchness," too much stress and stimulation. The term *stressed out* is appropriate. Stress may increase

DOI: 10.4324/9780429203640-8

incrementally, the straw that breaks the camel's back. Things may be going along reasonably well, but then one event after another begins to push the envelope toward anger. Any one, or two, or three of these issues might be easily handled, but too many of them piled up exceed the individual's tension-regulatory capacity and lead to anger. As discussed in the clinical illustration later in this chapter, these processes have important clinical implications for affect regulation.

It is interesting to note that any affect, positive or negative, if excessive enough, can produce anger. For example, too much excitement can lead to anger; if a decrease in stimulation (enjoyment) is too much, this can lead to boredom, irritability, and anger; a too-intense startle episode can result in fear and anger. Anger is also a final common pathway for all the negative affects. Excessive distress, fear, shame, disgust, and dissmell can all ultimately trigger an anger response. This is important clinically and in daily life, especially with respect to understanding anger that may have roots in excessive fear or shame.

Anger is also what might be termed a *contagious affect*—anger in one person can readily elicit anger in another. How and why? How—probably because someone else's anger adds to another's own level of distress. Think of a car honking behind you, or road rage. This increase in stimulation can feel like an attack, an assault, or a warning about your own behavior. Why contagious? Probably, from an evolutionary perspective, because anger in another person creates enough stimulation to elicit a startle response, or distress, or anger, in order to respond to a potential threat.

Although anger may be the basic affect, there are many words used to describe different aspects of anger. This can sometimes enhance or confuse the understanding of anger in clinical as well as everyday circumstances. Consider, for example, annoyance, irritability, hostility, rage, viciousness, aggression, and destruction.

Anger and Fear

Anger and fear are toxic affects. They are closely related in that they can each trigger the other and can be triggered by the other. In addition, they both have a powerful capacity to impair interest (see Chapter 4). The following daily-life vignette shows how anger and fear can interact in a very wounding manner. If anger and fear are used early and often, serious problems can result, both internally and in relationships.

My friend Carol told me of an episode that highlighted some of these issues. Her father was a rather irritable man, and Carol and her dad had never gotten along very well—due in large part to his fear for her welfare and the anger that resulted from this fear. One summer, when she was 18 years old, she was barefoot and using a power mower to cut the lawn by her house. Suddenly, she heard a noise next to her, a roar, which increased over the sound of the lawnmower. She looked over, startled, and saw her red-faced father yelling at her—"Carol, stop now! Stop! . . . Put your shoes on!" Carol was terrified. Her father was racked with fear and had morphed into rage. Unfortunately, neither of them had understood that his anger was the result of his fear for his daughter's safety—and his expression of rage was quite wounding to her. This was not an isolated incident, and his underlying caring feelings for her never made it past his fear and anger.

Some Clinical and Theoretical Issues

There are many psychological problems related to anger, including obsessive-compulsive disorders, paranoia, anxiety disorders, depression, delinquency, violence, and more. Some of these involve internalization of anger, and some involve behavioral expressions of anger.

Affect theory may be of use in understanding some of the various clinical issues involved with anger. Recall that affects can interact with each other and trigger each other. Excessive distress, shame, and disgust can trigger anger, and anger can trigger fear. Anger often brings with it loud noise, impulsivity, shame, pain and violence, loss of control, and violent fantasies.

In one sense, anger is supposed to alert the individual and the environment. The negative affects are signals for help, and anger conveys that something is really wrong. A major function of the mind is to create order and coherence (Basch, 1988; Demos, 2019), and anger can be destabilizing and disorganizing. However, in life-threatening situations or competition, anger may be very motivating and focusing.

Narcissistic rage, as discussed by Heinz Kohut, is a particular type of anger: It involves anger that is especially related to the affect of shame and a person's sense of self. It occurs when a person's sense of self, self-esteem, competence, or capabilities have been wounded or diminished—a narcissistic injury (Kohut, 1972). Kohut described this as "aggression as it arises from the matrix of a narcissistic imbalance" (p. 362) and an "insatiable search for revenge after a narcissistic injury" (p. 362). This can be the result of external provocation or internal self-abasement and incompetence. Narcissistic rage may involve a disruption of one's internal world, or it may be organized around a hated person or system (see Chapter 13).

The common psychodynamic defenses used to cope with anger include repression, disavowal, projection (often leading to paranoia), displacement, denial, withdrawal, externalization, and others. These defenses are apparent in "normal" development and, if excessive, in psychopathology.

The mutative factors in psychoanalysis and psychotherapy include interpretation (childhood antecedents, etc.) and various aspects of the patient-therapist relationship. With anger, one goal is to detoxify the anger, often by addressing the defenses and allowing the anger to see the light of day and to become able to talk about it. Much of this process includes enhancing interest, curiosity, and self-reflection so that the affect of anger can be explored and better understood—what and who triggers it, what images and fantasies occur, what it feels like in the body and face, and so on.

Verbalization is a crucial aspect of "working through," understanding, and detoxifying the anger. Verbalization allows for symbolization, communication, the use of metaphor, and articulation of unconscious affects, all of which can enhance capacities for self-reflection and tension-regulation. Many clinicians and theoreticians emphasize the importance of putting into words the various triggers, feelings, fantasies, and so on associated with anger. Anny Katan (1961), Judy Yanof (1996), Phyllis Tyson (2005), and John Gedo (2005) are among those who have contributed to our understanding of these processes (see Chapter 11).

Psychotherapeutic work with children and parents involves the affects of interest and anger. Interest is involved in the efforts to help both parents and children appreciate that the behaviors of children have meaning and are motivated by underlying feelings. The idea is to help the parents and children become curious about their feelings and actions and what triggers them.

The affect of anger often troubles parents the most. I have found two approaches particularly useful. One is to help parents and children understand the affect of anger as a quantitative issue—"too muchness," excessive distress, a call for help. The other is to focus on allowing the anger to be expressed (rather than inhibiting it) and then to put words to that process. This is similar to what a therapist tries to do with adult patients: working through the defenses as noted here and enhancing verbalization of the processes. This emphasis on interest, being curious, understanding anger, and verbalization also has a preventive as well as curative aspect in that it helps protect against developmental derailments and the formation of psychopathology.

Children's dreams and nightmares present another example of anger in the clinical arena. Cliff Wilkerson, a child psychoanalyst, wrote a remarkable and comprehensive article on children's dreams (1981). Children's dreams and nightmares can have a variety of antecedents and meanings—joy, excitement, hopes, accomplishments . . . and also trauma, fear, loss, separation, feelings of fragmentation and nonexistence, and the like. In nightmares, frequently, children's fear and anger are involved: the fear of someone's anger toward them and the fear of their own anger. For instance, children's repressed anger can readily be projected onto the "scary and dangerous monsters in the closet and under the bed." In this

Photo 7.1 Cliff Wilkerson
Source: Courtesy of Cliff Wilkerson

way, children rid themselves of the frightening, forbidden anger—it is the monsters who are dangerous and angry. Frequently, helping parents and children understand, express, and talk about anger can lead to a resolution of the nightmares as well as an enhanced understanding of their intrapsychic world and capacity to communicate with others.

Anger is also an important aspect of psychoanalytic and psychotherapeutic transference and countertransference reactions. In such cases, it can be beneficial for clinicians to become increasingly aware of their own anger, their own childhood antecedents, and the conscious and unconscious communications from the patient that may be contributing to mobilizing the therapist's reactions. Understanding anger from the perspective of affect theory can often be useful in sorting out the complexities associated with transference and countertransference reactions.

A Clinical Illustration and Discussion

The patient, Elliott, was a 42-year-old unmarried man who worked in a large industrial corporation. He sought treatment because of his increasing depression and sense of anxiety and tension, because of his inability to get married despite his having had several long relationships with women, and because of his frustrations getting ahead at work. Despite his good work ethic, intelligence, and already high position, he felt that his trouble dealing with his colleagues was keeping him from moving as high as he might.

Much of our early work in the analysis involved helping him sort out and understand his various feelings, with some improvement in his tension-regulation capacities. His mother, in particular, had been horribly confused about what feelings were what, leaving Elliott a hodgepodge of subjective states that he had no way of understanding. Now, about two years into the analysis, the nature of his anger had begun to attract more of his attention. He was wrestling with his competitive feelings and outbursts toward his colleagues at work, issues that had kept him from otherwise-deserved promotions. He was beginning to understand some of the current and earlier antecedents to his angry moods as well as his tendency to project his anger onto people in his external world, subsequently viewing them as hostile, sadistic competitors.

One day, about midway through the session, I shifted in my chair, and he burst out: "Goddamn it, there you go again, rustling around . . . just distracted . . . you don't give a shit . . ." We were learning, in what appeared to be aspects of negative maternal transference, that I was seen as being self-absorbed, easily distracted, disinterested, and not really concerned about him.

That day, I had not felt distracted, and I decided to focus on another aspect of the process. "Sometimes, if I move in my chair it seems to throw you, but other times it doesn't," I commented.

"Well . . . I think that's so," he said with less agitation. "I think, at times, I just seem to blow . . . everything seems so awful . . . and the slightest thing just puts me over . . . other times, I don't seem as disrupted."

I noted: "The straw that breaks the camel's back . . . perhaps sometimes you feel so hurt and vulnerable that my shifting around just makes everything 'too much' and all the distress and irritability turns into rage."

He began sobbing. "When I'd blow up, my mother would hit me and scream, 'You nasty mean little boy.' I always felt I was just a bad, awful person—somehow wrong, like nothing I did was right, who I was wasn't right." Now, as he began to understand how his distress could escalate to anger and rage—and how his anger was further exacerbated by his mother's misunderstanding of his affects—he became freer to tell me more directly about his angry feelings toward me.

Yet, as Elliott became less inhibited, in particular about his anger—that is, less fearful of, embarrassed by, and distressed by his anger—the process seemed to become more rather than less confusing. What emerged was an increased focus on his inner world—he seemed more attentive to his reactions, feelings, and dreams rather than talking about his various battles and problems in his external world. When I drew this change to his attention, he said that, somehow, his outside world was not so charged in the same way. "It's more peaceful in some ways but more confusing and troubling in others. I don't know who I am . . . but at least I'm not just defining myself by whatever battles I fight outside."

We began to explore aspects of his self that had been unable to emerge up until now—interests, tastes, and pace. A long-submerged interest in his physical prowess became more prominent. Elliott joined sports teams, did some coaching of children, and took some courses in communications and broadcasting with an eye to announcing professional sports. At one point, as he was talking about his excitement in these endeavors, he said that it seemed that I was bored as he was describing these things. When I asked him to elaborate, he blurted out: "It's more than you're bored . . . if I talk more about this stuff, you'll just mess it up . . . I really had fun playing in that ballgame the other day . . . and coaching the kids before it . . . and one of my teachers in announcing said I really have a feel and voice for the game, and he has some connections with possible jobs . . . but you're going to make fun of it . . . you'll wreck it!"

I asked, in the midst of his experiencing these intense feelings about my making fun of and wrecking his interests, if any other imagery came to mind. He became somber and tearful: "It seemed like my mom was always messing things up for me . . . I was a pretty good athlete when young—fast and agile—and it seemed she either ignored it or told me how unimportant it was . . . or made fun of the sports cards I was collecting when I was very young." Now, as we explored the transference, he described a sense that his interests and capacities were not appreciated or validated and that he and his interests were under assault. However, this involved not just issues between his mother and him but also the various reasons his mother apparently had to undermine him. It was complicated by a father who, paradoxically, emphasized the importance of doing what one was interested in but was, in fact, distant and often absent from the household with work concerns, a situation that enraged his wife and caused increasing hurt and disappointment in his little son.

This brief vignette might be discussed from a number of perspectives, but the focus here is on the psychology of affect, especially anger. Dealing with anger is often a crucial clinical challenge. Anger can elicit fear and other affects in both patient and therapist, and it may be difficult to mobilize the curiosity and empathy needed to understand the anger.

First, one of the most important payoffs from affect theory lies in our better understanding of the specific affects and their triggers in the microscopic work with a patient's subjective states. With Elliott, initial confusion about feelings was profound. When, as a little boy, he was interested and excited about something, his mother would tell him he was showing off or convey disapproval in some form. Thus, he increasingly linked pleasurable episodes of interest with a profound sense of shame and humiliation. When scared of something or hurt, he was told he was a scaredy-cat with nothing to be afraid of or that he was not hurt, so why be so upset?

In this way, his expressions of fear and distress were invalidated, and he was ultimately shamed if he expressed either of them. His rage built up. Anger was not understood as a signal that something was wrong and needed fixing; rather, anger was seen as evidence of hostility and dissatisfaction that needed to be squelched. Bottled up in this way, Elliott's anger erupted into severe tantrums. Much of the

Photo 7.2 John Gedo

early part of the analysis, then, involved interpreting and labeling, in an incremental fashion, his subjective feeling states, that is, his affects, his internal conflicts about them, and his reactions (Holinger, 1999).

As Gedo stressed, it "may be necessary to *name* for the patient the affective reactions the analyst succeeds in identifying through direct observation of nonverbal behaviors, thereby gradually eliminating an alexithymia [difficulty experiencing, identifying, and expressing emotions]" (2005, p. 153, emphasis in original). Childhood interactions and enactments with the analyst finally become encoded in symbolic verbal form (Gedo, 2005), that is, putting words to the patient's anger. Understanding, tolerating, regulating, labeling, and interpreting the specific affects in this fashion is also another way in which to appreciate the idea of a holding environment (Winnicott, 1963; Modell, 1976; Slochower, 1996).

Second, the dynamics of the affects of distress and anger are clinically useful and often misunderstood. Distress involves sustained stimulation that has increased above the individual's optimal level; anger is defined as being triggered by sustained and still increasing stimulation. Anger, then, is triggered not only by excessive distress but also by *any excessive affect*. Clinically, this not only aids us in appreciating the negative transference and rage as a signal of excessive distress, but it also alerts us to the need to dissect and interpret other affects that may be contributing to the anger. For example, fear and shame may be crystallized in rageful transference responses and need to be elaborated.

Third, the importance of the affect of interest and the various ways in which it is interrupted and interfered with are crucial. With Elliott, his capacity to identify and invest in his interests was initially massively defended against and inhibited. Ultimately, his humiliation and fear were mobilized in the transference (in the form of fantasies about how I would respond to his interest), and these feelings, in turn, were linked with childhood antecedents. At that point, surprising new interests took center stage. As Elliott's confusion, fear, and shame about his feelings began to dissipate, there was an increase in his curiosity about himself, his internal world, his feeling states, and his behaviors. His interest affect was now less constricted and less under the sway of condemnation, fear, and shame, resulting in an enhanced alliance and self-observing capacities (Holinger, 2008).

One important therapeutic goal involves generating in our patients a sense of curiosity about their internal world and feelings. That is, we want to mobilize the affect of interest to aid in dealing with negative affects, especially anger, fear, and shame—for example: "What am I angry about, and why?" "What am I afraid of, and why?" "What am I ashamed of, and why?" The mishandling of the interest affect early in development compromises the capacity of interest to help understand negative affects, contributing to repression and disavowal.

Conceptually, the affects of interest and enjoyment, and how they are responded to, appear central to self-esteem and the notion of self. Shame impedes interest and enjoyment and erodes self-esteem (Kohut, 1971, 1984; Morrison, 1989; Nathanson, 1992). The interference of the positive affects by negative affects often disrupts a person's sense of self. Indeed, as Knapp (1987) pointed out, Basch (1976) and others have begun to suggest that the meaning of "self" itself is usefully thought of in terms of affect and its development.

The issue of anger will be revisited later in this book when we explore the early verbalization of affect in the prevention and treatment of problems in infants and children (see Chapter 11). Affects will continue to be prominent throughout the rest of this book, given their profound influence on motivation, development, psychopathology, and various aspects of society. We move now from a focus on affects to the second of the three primary information processing systems—cognition.

Chapter 8

Emerging Cognition

Chapter Outline:

- Defining cognition
- Early—and often unrecognized—cognition
- Increasingly complex cognition develops in the context of human relationships
- Infants and young children are smarter than we think: Recent studies of cognitive processes
- Studying early cognitive processes
- Learning and education
- Dysfunction and disorders of cognition
- In summary

This chapter explores various aspects of cognition in early development, with a particular focus on 1) the development of cognition through human interactions and 2) recent studies of the remarkable cognitive capacities in infants and young children.

Defining Cognition

Similar to the term *affect*, *cognition* has many meanings, and there are a variety of ways of exploring it. The dictionary defines it as a process of knowing and perceiving, an individual's accumulation and use of knowledge about the world, both outside and inside of oneself. Reason, self-reflection, perception, thought, knowledge, memory, reality-processing, learning, empathy, predicting, and generalizing are all under the umbrella of cognition. Cognition can involve conscious or unconscious processes. In 1790, John Adams noted that while "passions are the gales," "reason holds the helm." Freud highlighted the power of the cognitive processes: "The voice of the intellect is a soft one, but it does not rest till it has gained a hearing . . . in the long run, nothing can withstand reason and experience" (1927, pp. 53–54).

Experts in development have expanded and refined those definitions. Cognition is integrated with affect. As Tomkins noted, "Affect can determine cognition at one time, be determined by cognition at another time, and be interdependent under other circumstances" (1981, p. 324). He defined the cognitive system as "perception, the motoric, and memory. These ... all process information in one or another of several different ways" (1992, p. 13). Language, as well as affect, can also significantly influence cognition through the acquiring and transmitting of information. In the mid-1990s, science journalist Daniel Goleman highlighted these emotional-cognitive interactions in his well-known book *Emotional Intelligence* (1995).

When thinking about thinking, a variety of problems arise. As Bertrand Russell put forth, "There are things which we thought we knew and don't know ... I think nobody should be certain of anything ... there's no short cut to knowledge" (1960, pp. 12, 17, 19).

How do we know what we think we know? The discipline of epistemology grapples with this question—the study of the nature and grounds of knowledge, especially with reference to its limits and validity. Perception, memory, and reason can readily be shown to be faulty systems, as classic as well as current work has demonstrated (e.g., Freud, 1901; Mercier & Sperber, 2017; Kahneman, 2011; Lewis, 2017). Psychodynamic theorists (e.g., Basch, 1988) struggle with the impact of unconscious affective processes on conscious cognitive functions. Unconscious motives can distort conscious perceptions and understandings.

The attempt to nail down the nature of cognitive processes has produced many studies and massive literature. Most of this is well-known (e.g., Piaget & Inhelder, 1969; Kagan, 1981; Tomkins, 1992). Jean Piaget was among the first to study the stages of cognitive development systematically. His findings will not be recapped here, but they are foundational. The expanding understanding of human biology has also shaped how cognition is defined. For instance, neurobiologists are

Photo 8.1 Jean Piaget

exploring the relationships between the cerebral cortex (and cognitive issues) and the amygdala (affects/emotions).

Early—And Often Unrecognized—Cognition

Cognition involves perception and the accumulation of knowledge, but at what developmental stage does a human being begin perceiving and putting two and two together? It turns out that human fetuses and babies relate to and interact with the world and people in utero, at birth, and, of course, well beyond.

The view of infants as passive and noninteractive, as being in a state of "normal autism"—these notions have been dramatically overturned in the past several decades (e.g., see Stern, 1985). One just has to recall newborns' innate responses to stimuli leading to interest, fear, or distress to appreciate this capacity for interaction and relatedness.

How have we come to this different understanding? First, there was a flood of research and clinical work on infants and young children in the middle and second half of the 20th century. Names such as Winnicott, Spitz, Ainsworth, Fraiberg, Greenspan, Emde, Kagan, Field, Demos, and others became well-known in the field. In his famous study on orphans, René Spitz (1945, 1965) showed years ago that even infants who had food and clean surroundings would deteriorate and sometimes even die if they did not have caregivers with whom to relate and interact.

Many aspects of this research coalesced in 1985 with Daniel Stern's brilliant integration of development and clinical psychoanalysis in *The Interpersonal World of the Infant: A View from Psychoanalysis and Developmental Psychology*. In this work, Stern dispelled the notion of the infant as passive and unrelated. Instead, Stern's infant is immediately socially related and interested. I discussed this previously in the chapters on affects, and I will explore it in more detail shortly. Unfortunately, although Stern's work is well-known in psychoanalytic and developmental circles, the general public tends to be unaware of his importance.

Increasingly Complex Cognition Develops in the Context of Human Relationships

Young children's capacities for cognition are significantly influenced by their human relationships and the environment. The quality of these relationships is dependent to a large extent on the affects involved. If the relationships are focused on interest (curiosity) and enjoyment, the acquisition of knowledge can be greatly enhanced. If the relationships are dominated by fear and shame, the acquisition of knowledge may be severely compromised.

So, how do these relationships, upon which much of cognition is dependent, occur? Infants express their affects through facial expressions, bodily movements, and vocalizations. They can express these affects almost from day one: interest, enjoyment, surprise, distress, anger, fear, shame, disgust (a reaction to noxious tastes), and dissmell (a reaction to noxious odors). Thus, they can clearly communicate with their caregivers and the rest of the environment very early on. And their caregivers respond to these communications—whether it is distress, enjoyment, or anger. The babies and their caregivers are relating.

How else do babies relate? Let's not forget how helpless infants are—they cannot walk or talk; they have little limb control and poor hand-eye coordination. So what do they do? What they have is a rather mature visual-motor system, as Daniel Stern points out. That is, they use their eyes and gaze as a way to relate. The face is a communication center par excellence. Infants can relate, engage, and communicate with their eyes and gaze. Babies can look directly into the eyes of their caregivers and explore (interest) with their eyes—or they can shut or avert their eyes, be glassy-eyed, and gaze past their caregivers. In these ways, they can either make direct contact with their caregivers or can cut off, reject, and protect themselves from contact. And then, as Stern puts it, "They can also re-initiate engagement and contact when they desire, through gazing, smiling, and vocalizing" (1985, p. 22). Thus, they can regulate the amount, timing, and duration of stimulation and interaction.

Infants are social beings. They are not passive blobs just waiting to grow up. They are sensitive to and respond to their environment. Using their expressions of feelings and their visual-motor system, they interact with and relate to their caregivers throughout their infancy, long before they can walk or talk. This builds their cognitive powers and shapes their self-knowledge and knowledge of the world around them.

Interacting with an environment that enhances an infant's natural curiosity and interest establishes a foundation for cognitive capacities and learning. In such an environment, infants and young children are eager to explore and learn—and it turns out they are remarkably smart and full of potential.

Infants and Young Children Are Smarter Than We Think: Recent Studies of Cognitive Processes

In the first part of this chapter, I explored the importance of the infant/child's relatedness in enhancing cognitive development. Now, I will examine some recent findings highlighting infants' early cognitive capacities. This is not intended as a comprehensive review but rather as examples of infants' abilities. In addition, this material is presented in order to emphasize the importance of supporting the affect of interest in the service of cognition. As Daniel Stern noted,

> From birth on, there appears to be a central tendency to form and test hypotheses about what is occurring in the world. Infants are constantly 'evaluating' in the sense of asking, is this different from or the same as that?
>
> (1985, p. 42)

Studying Early Cognitive Processes

Alison Gopnik, PhD, is at the center of enhancing our understanding of how babies and young children think and learn. "Even the youngest children know, experience, and learn far more than scientists ever thought possible," she noted (2010, p. 76). Gopnik, with her coauthors Andrew Meltzoff and Patricia Kuhl, wrote an engaging book on these issues, titled *The Scientist in the Crib: Minds, Brains, and How Children Learn* (1999). The authors discuss a variety of studies she and her colleagues have conducted over the years to show what goes on in the minds of infants and small children.

Here is a brief look at some of these experiments.

18-month-olds Can Understand Preferences in Other People That Differ From Their Own

Gopnik and her colleagues wondered if 18-month-olds (toddlers) could understand that "I might want one thing, whereas you want another" (2010, p. 78). How did they explore this? The experimenters gave the babies two bowls of food, one full of Goldfish crackers and one full of raw broccoli. All the babies preferred the crackers. Then:

> An experimenter showed . . . 18-month-olds a bowl of raw broccoli and a bowl of Goldfish crackers and then tasted some of each, making either a disgusted face or a happy face. Then she put her hand out and asked, "Could you give me some?" The 18-month-olds gave her broccoli when she acted as if she liked it, even though they would not choose it for themselves.
>
> (Gopnik, 2010, p. 78)

Photo 8.2 Alison Gopnik
Source: Courtesy of Alison Gopnik

This would suggest the toddlers had the capacity to understand another person's perspective—that is, the toddler differentiated herself from the experimenter's self—the beginning of self-and-object differentiation as well as empathy.

Gopnik also studied 14-month-olds. These younger children, after tasting the broccoli and Goldfish, always gave the experimenter what they—the children—liked ... the Goldfish crackers! This suggests a developmental change in this area as children get older.

Babies Understand the Relationship Between a Population and a Small Sample From That Population

In one study, an experimenter

> showed eight-month-old babies ... a box full of mixed-up Ping-Pong balls: for instance, 80 percent white and 20 percent red. The experimenter would then take out five balls, seemingly at random. The babies were more surprised (that is, they looked longer and more intently at the scene) when the experimenter pulled four red balls and one white out of the box—an improbable outcome—than when she pulled out four white balls and one red one.
>
> (Gopnik, 2010, p. 78)

Young Children Use Statistical Evidence, Probabilities, and Experiments to Determine Cause and Effect

Other experiments showed how preschoolers used probabilities to see how a machine worked.

> We repeatedly put one of the two blocks on the machine. The machine lit up two out of three times with the yellow block but only two out of six times for the blue one. Then we gave the children the blocks and asked them to light up the machine. These children, who could not yet add or subtract, were more likely to put the high-probability yellow block on the machine.
>
> (Gopnik, 2010, p. 79)

Interestingly, in some studies, children were actually better than adults in considering unusual possibilities and correctly finding the casual patterns. Gopnik and her colleagues showed four-year-olds and adults a machine

> that worked in an odd way, requiring two blocks on it together to make it go. The four-year-olds were better than the adults at grasping this unusual causal structure. The adults seemed to rely more on their prior knowledge that things usually do not work that way, even though the evidence implied otherwise for the machine in front of them.
>
> (p. 80)

Learning and Education

In this chapter, I have tried to suggest that cognitive processes and learning are quite active in infants and children. Infants learn much from verbalizations, and they also learn a great deal from nonverbal interactions—a process called *social referencing*. I will discuss this kind of learning in more detail when looking at bias and prejudice in Chapter 13.

So how about more formal educational programs—elementary school, middle school, high school, college? Might our three information systems add some depth to the conservative/progressive debate in education? That is, how much influence should students have with respect to what courses they take and subjects they study (Field et al., 1989)?

Some (the so-called conservative group) suggest it is most useful to expose the students to a wide range and, at times, in-depth study of basic courses, concepts, and principles: math, algebra, geometry, sciences, literature and poetry, foreign languages, art, music, history, and so on.

Others (the progressive segment) suggest a smaller amount of time in required courses in order to give students more time to develop their innate interests and talents. This group notes that some of the best math, science, and artistic/musical/literary minds are active in their younger years—why not let them "pursue their passions" more vigorously during those years?

In addition, much of what the middle, high school, and college students are really interested in involves introspection and their own development and character structure (their feelings, relationships, problems), and rare are the courses dealing with psychodynamic psychology, development, and clinical studies.

Finally, the progressive group notes that allowing more time for the students to immerse themselves in their own interests may decrease the boredom and rage seen in the school systems, thus enhancing school safety and decreasing violence (Cohen, 2021; Holinger, 2021). Boredom can be understood in terms of affects: Boredom involves a lack of interest and enjoyment. It is a form of distress. And as with any excessive negative affect, boredom can trigger anger.

I will not resolve these educational dilemmas here. However, utilizing the information gleaned from studies in development may enhance these discussions and policies.

Dysfunction and Disorders of Cognition

It is useful to consider how cognition can be compromised. In everyday situations, there are common dysfunctions of cognition. Optical illusions are only the easiest example. Eyewitness accounts of crime and identification are notoriously flawed. Mistakes in perception and memory can readily compromise cognition and reality-processing.

For instance, let me give you a fascinating example of these dysfunctions. In a long-term outcome study of adolescents during the 1960s and 1970s, Dan Offer and his colleagues studied various aspects of the lives of a cohort of "normal" adolescents (no evidence of psychopathology). More than 30 years later, they contacted the subjects again. The researchers asked them about their memories of various aspects of their feelings and lives during their adolescence. "Our data show that there is essentially no correlation between what our [adult] subjects thought and felt about their adolescence and what they actually thought and felt as adolescents" (Offer et al., 2004, p. 99). In other words, the subjects, who were in their 40s and 50s at follow-up, were often unable to recall accurately the feelings and thoughts they had as adolescents.

Clinical work also exposes disorders of cognition. The psychoanalyst John Gedo wrote a brief summary of some of these disorders.

> The most common forms encountered in psychoanalysis are magical thinking and obsessionality, which may occur together or separately. Delusions may temporarily appear as aspects of deep therapeutic regression in occasional analytic cases. A wide variety of more focal defects in cognition, such as a lack of a sense of humor, inability to grasp the implications of human transactions, or mistrust of one's sense of reality, generally result from specific early childhood deprivations.
>
> (2005, p. xiii)

In Summary

As you saw in the chapters on affect, interest and excitement are innate motivators for learning and exploratory activities. Gopnik, Stern, and others have documented the remarkable capacities young children possess for exploring their world. Through interest and investigation, children are actually discovering ideas and processes that relate to biology, physics, psychology, and other sciences, and they even use hypothesis testing, probability theory, and empathy in their cognitive development.

I will note a brief vignette:

> A boy about three years old was trying to get a big carton of milk out of the refrigerator. He dropped it, and the milk spilled on the floor. His mother came into the kitchen. She was a scientist. Her reaction? She got some paper towels and knelt on the floor with her son. Putting the towels in the milk, she said: "Let's see what happens . . . see the milk moves up the fibers, the towel absorbs the milk . . ." Of course, parents do not always have the time and energy to do this. But she recognized that it made more sense to elicit interest and enjoyment rather than be critical about the spilled milk and use fear and shame. Her son turned out to be a world-class scientist.

Recognizing children's early cognitive capacities vividly shows how important it is to enhance the interest affect rather than impairing it by using negative affects such as distress, anger, fear, and shame. This is the root of learning, discovering, and creating. This is the root of the emergence of an authentic sense of self (Winnicott, 1971). Can we enhance rather than inhibit curiosity? Can we elicit rather than impair children's sense of self? Can we elicit children's interests rather than impose ours on them?

A remarkable picture emerges from the recent research on cognition in infants and children. As Gopnik noted,

> Far from being unfinished adults, babies and young children are exquisitely designed by evolution to change and create, to learn and explore. Those capacities, so intrinsic to what it means to be human, appear in their purest forms in the earliest years of our lives.
>
> (2010, p. 81)

I turn now to the third piece of the information processing system—language.

Chapter 9

Language
Before Children Begin to Talk

Chapter Outline:

- So what is language?
- Language: Assets and liabilities
- Babies' early capacities
- Parents' capacities: How to use language to expand children's understanding of feelings
- Translating affects into words: Examples
- Why parents need to be able to label their own affects accurately, too

Chapters 9 and 10 deal with language. The major issue involves connecting words to affects, that is, the verbalization of affect. This occurs in parent-child interactions long before as well as after children begin to speak. In Chapter 9, I explore language before children talk, and then in Chapter 10 I look at the interaction of affects and language after children begin speaking. Chapter 11 integrates affect, cognition, and language, with an emphasis on: 1) verbalization of affects as it occurs in early development; 2) empathy; and 3) clinical work.

So What Is Language?

Let's keep it straightforward. *Language* is made up of words, their pronunciation, and the methods of combining them that are used and understood by a community. It functions as an audible and systematic tool for communicating ideas and feelings. *Writing* is the use of agreed-upon symbols that represent the sounds and meanings that make up a language. It is one of the most revolutionary advances of human beings. "Through his powers of intellect, articulate language has been evolved; and on this his wonderful advancement has mainly depended" (Darwin, 1874, p. 49).

Acquisition of language impacts—and is impacted by—an individual child's development. It shapes expression and perception of positive and negative affects and cognition, and it can both enhance and complicate the capacities of affect and cognition as information processing systems.

DOI: 10.4324/9780429203640-10

When we talk about the importance of language, we almost automatically think in terms of when children begin to speak. But long before children speak, they are listening and seeing—and understanding far more than we used to think. "Infant" means incapable of speech—but it does not mean incapable of understanding speech.

Interestingly, researchers and clinicians who deal in detail with early parent-infant interactions now question if there is any "nonverbal" period of development (Vivona, 2012, 2014; Salomonsson, 2014). Why? Because the baby is immersed in words as well as sounds from pregnancy onward. So, the idea is that words and feelings combine very early on.

Language: Assets and Liabilities

As the infant researcher Daniel Stern (1985) reminds us, language creates tremendous advantages. "By the time babies start to talk they have already acquired a great deal of world knowledge" (p. 168). Language allows for them to express their emotions and

> shared meanings . . . The possible ways of 'being with' another increase enormously . . . In addition, it permits two people to create mutual experiences of meaning that have been unknown before and could never have existed until fashioned by words.
>
> (p. 162)

However, there are also liabilities. Language can be used for sharing, but since the same words can mean different things to different people, misperceptions and confusion can readily occur. Language and meaning become "something to be negotiated between the parent and child" (p. 170).

It is important to acknowledge the potential confusion caused by language when discussing the necessity of parents putting words to infants' or children's emerging feelings. If caregivers understand the children's expressions of interest, enjoyment, distress, anger, fear, and so on—and label them accurately with words—youngsters have a much better chance of understanding their own internal world and feelings. When children begin to be able to understand their own feelings accurately, it not only enhances their self-esteem but also enhances their capacity for empathy. Anny Katan describes this process beautifully—that of helping children connect feelings with words (Katan, 1961; see Chapters 10 and 11).

In contrast, if parents misunderstand or mislabel the affects, internal confusion and impaired interpersonal skills can result. For example, perhaps the child is in pain (distress—say from a splinter) to the point of being angry, and the parent doesn't realize the anger is an SOS signal asking for help with the pain. A squabble may result ("Don't you get angry with me!"), rather than a focus on the injury.

Babies' Early Capacities

Patricia Kuhl's research is stunning in demonstrating the ability of very young humans to master languages.

> An infant child possesses an amazing, and fleeting, gift: The ability to master a language quickly. At six months, the child can learn the sounds that make up English words and, if also exposed to Quechua and Tagalog, he or she can pick up the unique acoustic properties of those languages, too.
>
> (2015, p. 66)

Kuhl also notes the amazing openness of the infant brain:

> At birth, the infant brain can perceive the full set of 800 or so sounds, called phonemes, that can be strung together to form all the words in every language of the world ... The time when a youngster's brain is most open to learning the sounds of a native tongue begins at six months for vowels and at nine months for consonants.
>
> (Kuhl, 2015, p. 65)

At first, then, children may understand what is being communicated through tone of voice, inflection, gestures, facial expressions, and words. Studies have shown

Photo 9.1 Patricia K. Kuhl
Source: Courtesy of Patricia K. Kuhl

that soothing words and tones register differently to an infant than distressed and angry sounds or words. And it is also striking to realize how quickly very young children understand the meaning of words themselves.

From the earliest days of their lives, children are developing their vocabulary. In infancy, a child's ability to understand words far outstrips their ability to speak words. This is one reason it makes good sense to talk a lot with very young children; they are learning words and meanings long before they can speak. This becomes important: Parents putting words to feelings can enhance introspection, tension-regulation, and self-soothing, as I will discuss further in Chapter 11 (Katan, 1961; Holinger, 2016).

Parents' Capacities: How to Use Language to Expand Children's Understanding of Feelings

A child is never too young to understand what's going on (even if on a purely emotional level), and it is never too early to talk with a child. But questions arise: What kind of talk? What words? To what end? Almost any talking and words can be a useful learning experience for your child. But an especially useful strategy for the preverbal child is labeling her feelings with words accurately. The payoff is terrific if words for feelings can be brought into the conversations at the earliest possible time.

Parents can help young children become aware of their feelings (and feel that the parents "get them") by using the words for the affects when the opportunity presents itself. Consider these statements and how much they convey:

- "You seem *excited* about the glitter make-up!"
- "Perhaps you were *scared* when the dog ran up so fast?"
- "Maybe you were *distressed* and *angry* when I said no more cookies before dinner."

Translating Affects Into Words: Examples

During this discussion of language and affect, I will highlight the important back-and-forth oscillating process going on between affect and words. Here's an example of putting words to feelings before the child can talk.

Say your infant daughter is crawling toward a toy and accidentally puts her hand on a sharp thumbtack. Her eyebrows will arch in the middle, the corners of her mouth will drop down; her chin will begin to quiver; she may begin crying and then getting red in the face and howl. Upon seeing or hearing this, you will probably come over, pick her up, say something like "Oh, sweetheart; I'm so sorry," reassure her, hold her, and perhaps kiss her hand where it hurts.

What have you done here? You have correctly perceived that the thumbtack triggered your daughter's distress, fear, and then possibly excessive distress and angry feelings. You responded by attending to the trigger of her pain, getting rid of the thumbtack, kissing the hurt hand, and comforting her.

In this instance, you have understood your daughter's reactions—her facial expressions and cries are expressions of distress, fear, and anger. Many parents are able to do this instinctively—understand what feelings their baby is expressing through facial expressions and cries. Some parents are also aware of the existence of the innate affects and are able to translate the expressions into words at the time: "Oh, dear, that hurt, didn't it? I can see you are distressed and scared."

Let's look at another example. Your little boy is crawling on the floor and spots a small red car. He picks it up and looks at it intensely, with his eyebrows a bit down and his mouth slightly open. Now, he begins to play more actively with it, gurgling delightedly as he runs it back and forth along the floor. You realize he is interested in the little car, and he is getting excited as he plays with it. Technically, the affect of interest has been triggered—exactly what you want. You might even put it into words for him: "You sure seem *interested* in that car—that's great! You really are *excited*!"

This is the earliest kind of labeling of affects—moving from facial expressions and vocalizations into feelings.

It is a thrill when parents realize how much a child is processing and learning before she utters her first word. Finally, they can talk to their child and be clearly understood. "Please bring your shoes to me so we can put them on" . . . and lo and behold, the child gets his sneakers. "Will you please pick up your trains from the floor so no one steps on them and breaks them?" And she picks up her trains. The child may not be able to speak yet, but she is accumulating an understanding of many, many words—far more than she will be able to put voice to for months and months.

Why Parents Need to be Able to Label Their Own Affects Accurately, Too

There is also extensive literature in experimental psychology that tends to support the efficacy of putting words to feelings, particularly as a viable form of emotional regulation. Studies have found that verbalization (spoken or written) of current emotional experience reduces distress, in contrast to no verbalization, verbalization of nonaffective material, distraction, or reappraisal (Frattaroli, 2006; Kircanski et al., 2012; Pennebaker & Chung, 2011; Torre & Lieberman, 2018). Also, neuroimaging studies suggest that affect labeling diminishes the response of the amygdala and enhances the activity of the cortex (Lieberman et al., 2007). This leads to greater self-reflection, use of reason, and impulse regulation.

In addition, some research suggests that parents' capacity to link words and feelings is a crucial aspect of good parent-child relationships and healthy development of the child's personality. Anny Katan described this process dramatically in her clinical work with parents and children (1961). She noted some parents not only had difficulty understanding and showing their own emotions, but they also tended to inhibit the showing of emotions in their children.

Greg Lowder and his colleagues explored this issue in an intriguing set of studies, highlighting the significance of the parent being able to put affects into words. They eloquently summarized the work as follows:

> Many factors come to bear on how successfully a mother will be able to manage the parenting experience. A primary factor may be her (mother's) ability to connect her emotions to language. Her ability to do so, more or less successfully, will affect her capacity to regulate emotions as they arise, along with her ability to receive support from others by successfully communicating what she feels.
>
> (2007, p. 266)

In the next chapter, we will explore language—and its interactions with affects and cognition—when children begin to talk.

Chapter 10

Affects Into Words
When Children Begin to Talk

Chapter Outline:

- Beginning to talk
- Example #1—Ben at one year old ... and then two years old
- Example #2—Josh: Confusion and rejection
- Example #3—Preschooler in therapy
- Language beyond early childhood
- Interaction of words and feelings: Wilbur and Orville Wright

> With the simultaneous emergence (at around 18 months) of language, of evocative (recall) memory, internal imaging, and fantasy, the child becomes a different being.
> —Barbara Fajardo, PhD, 1987, p. 235.

Beginning to Talk

When a child begins to talk, some fascinating changes begin to occur. Some of these changes involve the internal world of the child, such as increased capacities for self-reflection and symbolic play (Stern, 1985). Other changes involve interpersonal interactions. All three information processing systems undergo changes when the child becomes verbal.

The toddler years provide spectacular opportunities for enhancing intellectual and emotional development. Language is a large part of this, opening up an entirely new world of growth during the early years. I once overheard a toddler with a new toy saying, "I am excited, ecstatic, exuberant!" Another time, I saw a father point out a puppy to his four-year-old daughter and say, "Just think, that puppy was in its mother's tummy just a few weeks ago!" ... And his daughter said, "Uterus, Daddy, uterus!"

Language represents a huge developmental leap. We can communicate and share complex thoughts, feelings, ideas, and perceptions. Yet, language can distort as well as enhance—people often bring different meanings and experiences to words (Stern, 1985). And, as linguist and psychoanalyst Bonnie Litowitz notes, language also provides the means by which we can sort out our misinterpretations (2014).

DOI: 10.4324/9780429203640-11

I still remember the time my son said his first word. We were in the kitchen. He looked up over the counter, saw some fruit, and said "ap-ple." I was stunned, then joyful—and surprisingly oblivious, at that moment, to the enormous and inspiring power that had been unleashed.

When children speak their first words, there is often a sense of relief. For months and months after a baby is born, parents struggle to understand the various noises, gestures, and expressions an infant uses to express needs, feelings, and thoughts. It's a great thrill when you and your child are beginning to function in the same reality, one shaped by words.

So, as the child begins to talk, you may think, "Ah, this is getting so much easier." And in some ways, this makes sense. Words are a great tool. But like all tools, they can be used to build things up or tear them down. As children begin to talk, these words can seem as much like a sledgehammer as anything else.

Many months after my son first said, "Ap-ple," he'd expanded his vocabulary to include somewhat more hefty words, such as "No" and "I no like you!" I confess at that point, I may have felt a little less joyous. A parent's job—opportunity—is to translate the terse, word-limited, unnuanced expressions and actions of a toddler into more precise expressions of feelings, desires, and ideas. And that can be done using the back-and-forth process of changing words into affects and affects into words.

As children grow up—at around age two—they change how they give life to their feelings. The facial expressions they used so actively as infants, while still there, are joined by early words.

Once a child begins to talk, the task of helping a child learn to use words to express feelings appropriately —the whole gamut from joy to rage—can bring many and immediate rewards. Anny Katan, MD, a child psychoanalyst, commented eloquently on the benefits of encouraging word use and talking in a child

Photo 10.1 Anny Katan

(1961). She suggested that verbalization increases the possibility of distinguishing between fantasy and reality. If the child can verbalize his feelings, he can learn to delay action (such as a tantrum). The idea is "words, not actions." Verbalization leads to the integration of affects, cognition, and language, which in turn results in reality-processing and enhanced self-understanding. This nicely sums up the benefits of encouraging words—and putting affects into words, as discussed in more detail in Chapter 11.

Example #1—Ben at One Year Old . . . and Then Two Years Old

Ben, a year old, and his mother are in the kitchen. Ben is in his highchair playing with a little toy car and having a snack. The car falls off and onto the floor. Ben begins to get distressed (mouth turned down, eyebrows arched). Mom can't get to the car right away and says: "Hold on, Ben, I'll get your car in a sec." Ben relaxes a bit; he knows he has been understood, and he looks forward to seeing the results. He's really interested in the car, and when his mom takes a few seconds too long (in his view of things) to retrieve the car for him, his distress returns full blast. Then, his distress morphs into anger. His face turns red, and he lets out a cry of despair. Mother hears this, puts down the pan she's working on, and says: "Okay, okay, I get it . . . here, Ben, here's the car," as she picks it up and hands it to him. Ben takes the car, smiles, and goes "vroom, vroom" as he runs it across his highchair table.

Skipping ahead a year, Ben, now two years old, is in the highchair, playing with a car. It falls on the floor. "Car, car, car down," he says, asking for a response. Mom hears these words as a bit demanding but maintains her cool: "Just a second, honey, I've got my hands full." Ben brightens at her voice, but then, when some time goes by, he gets more distressed: "Car, car!" he yells.

Mom, unconsciously reacting to the verbal response as she might to anyone who was talking *at* her, says, "Hold on, I'll be there; just wait a minute." But to Ben, yelling "car, car" is just like letting out a cry of distress. If that is not responded to as it was when he was preverbal, he gets even more frustrated and angry. He expresses his distress by trotting out the limited vocabulary he has at his disposal: "No, no! I no like you . . . I hate you!"

This can be devastating to a parent. The sweet, needy, tender infant has turned into a nasty monster! These words may seem to be much more of a personal attack than the preverbal wailing that Ben's mom (and all parents) was used to. So, in the second example, Ben's mom feels put upon and assaulted. She doesn't like what she is hearing in words. She doesn't like the word "hate." She snaps at him: "Ben, stop it! We don't talk like that in this house." And the battle is joined. You can fill in the blanks: Ben throws his food on the floor. Mom gets angry. Ben yells and says more. A timeout is declared.

What happened? The complexity of language has emerged! As the example of Ben and his mother illustrates, language brings with it a remarkable set of reactions on the part of parent and child. On the plus side, language ushers in many positive results: Words give children a way to enhance communication and increase their capacity for understanding and regulating feelings. When a word is put to a feeling, children gain power over that feeling; there is an increasing ability to examine and mold it, to share or modify it, or to enjoy it or to let it go. But, there is also the opportunity for distortion and miscommunication, which can lead to conflict. Language has become a double-edged sword.

With the nonverbal Ben, his mother was able to recognize the distress and anger, and she fixed what had triggered those feelings by reassuring him and then picking up the car. Ben's expression of his distress and anger did not throw her off. However, when Ben became verbal, using words such as "no like" and "hate," his mother lost her bearings. She had trouble understanding that Ben was expressing exactly the same feelings as before: distress and anger. But when these feelings were crudely put into words, language itself threw a monkey wrench into their communication.

Is there a way out of this dilemma? Yes—connect the affects to the words. There are a variety of expressions that can be used to describe this back-and-forth process of feelings and words: verbalization, affective labeling, and symbolic encoding. Regardless of how one articulates it, this process is one of oscillations between affects and words.

Before an infant can talk, the parent tries to decipher and put words to the affects behind the infant's use of facial expressions, vocalizations, and behaviors. After a child begins to talk, the affects-to-words process becomes more back and forth. As a toddler begins to use words, these words are often quite raw and primitive—and the process involves labeling the child's words with the words for affects. So the toddler's words or actions—"no" or "hate" or "gimme, gimme"—get reworked into the affects that underlie the words: "distress" or "anger" or "excited." It is the affects that are the prime motivators of the child's actions and words. It is this interplay between affects, actions, and words that underlies all psychotherapy and psychoanalysis of people of any age. Winnicott (1958, 1965b), Salomonsson (2006, 2014), and others have beautifully described these processes in working with parents, infants, and young children. This interplay between affects and words will be discussed in more detail later (also see the clinical example in Chapter 7 on anger).

Example #2—Josh: Confusion and Rejection

A family comes home from a nice vacation, during which the father has spent lots of time with his three-year-old son Josh; they have so much fun being with each other. After the first day back, the father comes home from work and goes to hug his son hello. His son reacts negatively, pulling away, saying, "No kiss, I no like you . . . go away!"

What's happening here? Let's go back to the basics. What feelings underlie the words "no kiss," "no like," "go away"? Distress and anger are the feelings. So why is the little boy distressed? Because he missed his dad! He felt left and abandoned by his dad after they had spent all those nice vacation days together.

With this understanding of the feelings behind the words, father and son can begin to sort out the problem. Father can take a breath and try to say something like: "I think you're distressed and angry at me . . . maybe you can say 'I am angry at you' . . . I think you're angry at me and wanted me to go away because I hurt your feelings. I disappointed you. I left you this morning after all those days of fun together! And I loved our time together! I'm sorry I had to leave you and go to work this morning."

Children can understand such seemingly sophisticated ideas and feelings; in fact, they long for them. Validation and understanding are vital if children are to feel that they matter, that their emotions have a place in the world and that they are loved for who they are.

When you put a word to a child's feelings and take the time to explore what is going on, you are essentially translating from toddler speak to adult speech. This is most effectively done by labeling the feelings, especially if you use the actual names of the nine affects—interest, fear, enjoyment, and so on. Or use variations: "I think that scared you" or "that little car really excited you." Or get playful with synonyms: "You sure are interested and excited . . . and elated, exuberant, ecstatic!"

Children learn much faster than we think they do. They can readily learn these words. And when children learn words for feelings, they are doing what is termed *symbolically encoding* their internal feeling states (Gedo, 2005). This allows for increased thoughtfulness, self-reflection, and decreased impulsivity. For instance, a child who begins to label her tantrums as feelings of "distress" and then "anger" becomes increasingly capable of recognizing the sequences involved in the tantrums, what triggered them, whether she was feeling "very distressed" and "very angry" or less so.

"Label the feelings" or "put words to the feelings" become the mantras. A child who is able to label her feelings as "interested" or "excited" or "angry" or "scared" has a huge head start on her tension-regulation capacity, that is, her capacity (conscious and unconscious) to manage her various anxieties and feelings and to calm herself down when she gets anxious or frustrated. This will be explored further with a clinical example in the next chapter.

Learning to control ourselves when challenged by the outside world is an ability that has lifelong benefits. For example, teens who learn this early are better able to think before they act, and they can stand up for themselves in the face of peer pressure much more effectively. That is where the environment and inner world of the child come together.

Example #3—Preschooler in Therapy

I was seeing a four-year-old girl who was having a lot of trouble adjusting to preschool. When she returned home from school, her parents said she would be angry and difficult to communicate with. She often threw tantrums and called her mother names. She swore at her, which upset her mother enormously. The only thing that seemed to calm the little girl down was if her mother would read to her. But the mom would get so mad at the way her child was behaving that she would refuse to read to her until she calmed down. The very tool at the mother's disposal for helping her child was used to try to bludgeon her into "good" behavior. The results were dismal.

By showing the mom that the child's acting out was a cry for quiet time together, not an assault on the mother or her parenting abilities, the mom was able to gain control of her own emotions. She was able to talk with her daughter about what was upsetting her at school and to find a way to enjoy reading to her child for about ten minutes, a little soothing ritual, after school every day. The trick was not to get caught up in the child's expression of a strong negative emotion but to hear all this as an SOS signal—and to translate, understand, and help the child with whatever triggered the feelings. Then the mother could realize that the reading was a soothing mechanism for her daughter—and for her too. She began to use the reading as a tension-regulator for both of them. This, in turn, helped the little girl strengthen her own self-soothing capacities.

Language Beyond Early Childhood

Up to now, language has been discussed primarily in the context of infancy and early childhood. It is time now for a brief mention of language in the larger scope of individual development and ages beyond childhood.

Language, as we have seen, has profound assets and liabilities. Sometimes, misinterpretations seem inevitable. However, as Bonnie Litowitz notes,

> The use of language to talk about language allows us to discover if we are indeed "getting the message," are "on the same page" . . . As we strive to understand

Photo 10.2 Bonnie Litowitz
Source: Courtesy of Bonnie Litowitz

our patients, we are constantly trying to understand the nature and possible causes of our misinterpretations.

(2014, p. 302)

Just as affects and cognition morph into greater complexity with age, so also does language. Language achieves greater sophistication, and this can create opportunities for greater subtleties. However, these changes can also create distance from the innate affects themselves—to estrange a person from his or her innate, unfiltered feelings. Despite these developments, the importance of the previously described oscillations remains between affects, actions, and words.

Throughout life, language use and meaning change. The young child may say: "I hate you . . . I no like you!" That is pure *distress* and *anger* before the subtleties and sophistication of more adult language shape their expression.

Adolescents use language in often bewildering ways, too. But their meanings are clear—just as a child's are—if you connect the dots between the actions and words and affects. For example, a 15-year-old is waiting for the train and becomes bored (distressed), not excited. He begins fooling around with various luggage tags on a pile of suitcases on a cart. His parents finally get upset and tell him to stop. Snippiness and arguments follow. So what's happening here? The stimulus-seeking brain is doing just what it is supposed to do—and the teenager is bored! Interest and enjoyment are not being triggered. The answer is easy—translate back to the need for interest and enjoyment. What reading, games, music, or activities might be of interest?

One sees this scenario all the time—in smaller children (at restaurants or grocery stores), adolescents, and adults. The priority seems to be an understanding of the affects underlying the behaviors.

This discussion of the oscillations of words and affects leads me into the clinical arena, which will be discussed in more detail in the next chapter. The effectiveness of psychotherapy and psychoanalysis involves the patient-therapist relationship and understanding the patient's internal world. The key constant in working with patients is trying to understand the underlying feelings—the feelings that exist, consciously or unconsciously, behind a patient's words and actions. It is in helping people understand what they are feeling and why, what they are interested in, and what they are distressed by, that gets them on track.

Interaction of Words and Feelings: Wilbur and Orville Wright

Before closing this chapter on language, consider this remarkable example of the interaction of words and feelings in a letter Wilbur Wright wrote to an old mentor and friend, Octave Chanute, in 1910 after they had a falling out:

My brother and I do not form many intimate friendships, and do not lightly give them up. I believed that unless we could understand exactly how you felt, and you could understand how we felt, our friendship would tend to grow weaker instead of stronger. Through ignorance or thoughtlessness, each would be touching the other's sore spots and causing unnecessary pain. We prize too highly the friendship which meant so much in the years of our early struggles to willingly see it worn away by uncorrected misunderstandings, which might be corrected by a frank discussion.

(McCullough, 2015, p. 250)

This increasing interaction of affects, cognition, and language leads to the next chapter, in which we explore early verbalization of affects, empathy, and some clinical implications.

Chapter 11

Integrating Affects, Cognition, and Language

The Impact of Early Verbalization of Affects, the Emergence of Empathy, and Clinical Implications

Chapter Outline:

- Early verbalization of affects
- Empathy: Definitions and functions
- Four clinical cases
- The impact of words: Feelings, actions, and interpersonal skills

In this chapter, I will explore various aspects of integrating affects, cognition, and language, developmentally and clinically. I start with the remarkable impact that early verbalization has on development. Next, I turn to empathy, which stems from an integration of the three information systems. And finally, I will present several clinical cases that highlight work with troubled children. These provide examples of the integration of affects, cognition, and language, with the goals of enhancing potential and preventing problems.

Early Verbalization of Affects

From birth, parents and children start an interesting, oscillating, back-and-forth process: First, the parents verbalize their children's feelings, observations, and actions—hopefully with some accuracy and empathy. As children acquire spoken language, they erratically and often with unintended bluntness verbalize their affects, emotions, and observations. The parents are then challenged to translate these unpolished word choices for themselves and for their children in an effort to decrease misinterpretations. And, finally, children (hopefully) become more and more able to verbalize affects and emotions accurately, a process of refinement that continues for a lifetime.

This process of parental integration of a child's affects and language can enhance development (e.g., communication, interpersonal skills, self-understanding) and help prevent developmental and emotional problems in the child by, for example, nurturing tension-regulation. Years ago, outside of a clinical setting, I noted an interesting example of early verbalization of affect in action. A three-and-a-half-year-old was playing vigorously and then announced: "I am excited, ecstatic, elated!" It turned out his parents had been intrigued with helping him put words to his feelings. What had they done here? They were integrating affects, cognition, and language, using their understanding of their child's feelings and combining that with the child's increasing cognitive capacities and language acquisition. As a result, both the parents and the child had an enhanced awareness of their own feelings and those of each other. This brings us to a short yet important paper by Anny Katan (1961).

Anny Katan, a child psychoanalyst, was born in Vienna, Austria, and she moved to Cleveland after WWII. There, she established a remarkable child treatment center, now called the Hanna Perkins Center for Child Development. She published a paper in 1961 titled "Some Thoughts about the Role of Verbalization in Early Childhood." Based on her extensive work with parents and young children, Katan wanted to emphasize specifically "the importance of the verbalization of feelings by the very young child" (p. 185).

Katan made three important points. First, she noted that verbalization of perceptions of the outer world proceeds verbalization of feelings: "Usually the child is not so quick at learning words to express the inner perceptions of his feelings" (1961, p. 185). The child perceives feelings and expresses some without words—crying, laughing, facial expressions, body movements. However, here is the main point: "These feelings are not usually given names. Often they are not understood by the parents . . . the task of parents is much more difficult. *They have to guess at the child's feelings*" (p. 185, emphasis added).

Katan's second and third points derived from her first—the importance of early verbalization of feelings. Her second finding was that verbalization led to an increased mastery of self-control, that is, not acting on feelings immediately but instead mobilizing greater self-reflection and delaying action. Interestingly, she noted that "we found that they [the children] demonstrated a mastery of their feelings and that this mastery led secondarily to a feeling of greater security" (1961, p. 187). Third, Katan suggested that verbalization aided in "distinguishing between wishes and fantasies on the one hand, and reality on the other . . . to differentiate between pretend and real" (p. 188)—in other words, the child's capacity for reality-processing is enhanced. Katan summarizes: "Thus, through verbalization, the ego is able to master its affects and does not have to resort to defenses like denial, avoidance, etc., to shut these affects out" (p. 188). I want to note here that Katan is encouraging the verbalization of negative as well as positive affects.

In addition, Katan also stressed the importance of working with the parents as well as with the children. Parents may often be unable to verbalize their own feelings accurately, and this affects their children—both in the children's ability to accurately use words to describe their own feelings and in their ability to empathize.

> I have in mind the type of parents who not only are unable to show their own emotions, but also do not permit emotions to show in the child. If such parents speak about their feelings, which they are unable to show, or speak about the

child's feelings, it is clear that their words are used not to further the expression of emotions but to ward emotions off. If this is the case, the words are not a bridge, as they ought to be, but are a defense against the emotions.

(1961, p. 187)

Working with both children and parents enhances the capacities of all involved to verbalize and understand their feelings and internal worlds, with gains in self-reflection, impulse regulation, and empathy.

This brief paper by Katan in 1961 implicitly brings together affects, cognition, and language. Subsequent to this, there have been tremendous advances in our understanding of early development and the three information processing systems. These advances have made it possible to enhance therapeutic efforts with infants and parents (e.g., Fraiberg et al., 1975; Stern, 1985; Salomonsson, 2014; Vivona, 2012, 2014; Kuhl, 2015); children and adolescents (Fonagy & Target, 1996a; Novick & Novick, 2005; Hoffman et al., 2016); and adult psychotherapy and psychoanalysis (Kohut, 1971, 1984; Modell, 1976; Pine, 1990; Basch, 1988; Gedo, 2005).

Empathy: Definitions and Functions

Affect, cognition, and language are intimately connected with the concept of empathy: all are involved in the capacities needed for empathy and for the conveying of empathy. *Empathy* implies being aware of, being sensitive to, and vicariously experiencing another's feelings, thoughts, motives, and experiences; empathy does not include judgment of those feelings. Empathy is often fueled by curiosity, that is, the affect of interest.

Empathy became an increasingly important topic with Heinz Kohut's work and the emergence of self-psychology in the second half of the 20th century. Empathy has a large literature—it has been discussed in detail by Kohut (1959, 1966, 1971), Basch (1983a, 1988), and many others. They address a complicated question: How does empathy occur?

Kohut suggested that empathy is

accomplished by introspectively gaining direct access to our ideation, to our feeling states, to our tensions, our affects, and to those of others via vicarious introspection . . . by the use of a variety of cues that we obtain, and on the basis of the essential similarity between people, we can with some hope of correctness and accuracy grasp what another person feels, experiences, thinks.

(Tolpin & Tolpin, 1996, p. 350)

Kohut also brought up the advantages and complexities that language brings to the issue:

Communication by language is, of course, one way in which this particular type of vicarious introspection is furthered. Somebody tells us what he feels;

then we know what he feels. Or we take it with a grain of salt, since he may not be telling us the truth. That kind of thing. The methodology of the introspective, empathic observation of the psychological universe is another story. It needs as many, if not more, safeguards than those we use in appraising verbalized statements.

(p. 350)

Basch conveys the relevance of including affect, cognition, and language as all contributing to what we call empathy. He also highlights the importance of Tomkins's accurate identification of affects and the significance of putting language to the affects (1976; Katan, 1961). But he does not stop there. He proposes that empathy is a part of a developmental process involving affect. Basch suggests the term *affect* be used for the subcortical visceral and vascular reactions, as discussed previously. He uses the term *feeling* when affective reactions begin to be related to a concept of self, around 18–24 months. *Emotion* refers to the joining together of feeling states with experience to give meaning to our more complex concepts such as love, sadness, and happiness. Basch proposes the "final maturational step in affective development is the capacity for *empathic understanding*—that is, affective communication that goes beyond the self-referential" (1988, p. 78, emphasis in original).

Empathy, the ability to put oneself in the place of another, represents, I believe, the final potential transformation of affective communication. On the level of cognitive operations, empathy depends on *decentering*, a term used by Piaget (Piaget & Inhelder, 1969) to describe the ability to take an objective view toward one's own self through both reflection and what Vygotsky called *inner speech*.

(Basch, 1983a, pp. 118–119)

Photo 11.1 Michael Franz Basch
Source: Courtesy of Gail Basch, MD

Empathy and the Clinical Arena

Beginning with his 1959 paper ("Introspection, Empathy, and Psychoanalysis—An Examination of the Relationship Between Mode of Observation and Theory"), Kohut used the concept of empathy to focus on the self, narcissistic problems, and disorders of the self. From this, he described a different way of exploring, understanding, and treating these patients. He ultimately suggested alternative ways of viewing their development and the transferences that resulted (1966, 1971, 1977, 1984; Tolpin & Tolpin, 1996).

Basch elaborated on the nature of empathy in the therapeutic setting:

> It often requires from us a long period of listening to what the patient is saying (or not saying), examining our own reactions to this material analytically, and then bridging the gap between ourselves and the patient by constructing suitable analogies between his associations and our own experiences, before we finally may find ourselves attuned to the patient's affective communications.
>
> (1983a, p. 112)

Ralph Greenson (1960) described his understanding of the empathic process in analysis as one of immersion over time:

> I listened to the patient's words and transformed her words into pictures and feelings from *her* memories and *her* experiences and in accordance with her ways ... The events, words, and actions the patient described were now permitted to permeate the working model. The model reacted with feelings, ideas, memories, associations, etc.
>
> (p. 421, emphasis in original)

Empathy in Other Situations

Up to now, empathy has been discussed primarily in terms of one person trying to understand the feelings and motives of another—i.e., therapist and patient. What about people who want to be empathized with, who want someone else to understand them? In a sense, this is what evolution has done for infants. Negative affects are SOS signals for the caregivers—distress, fear, and anger. It is as if the babies are saying, "Ouch!" And the parents need to be able to hear the meanings behind the affect and translate these affects into meanings, into words—"I need help. I am in trouble. Can't you see how I feel?" This is what Katan describes as so crucial: the connecting of the affects with language (1961).

There is another situation seen in children and adults in which individuals or groups try to force others to empathize with them. This may occur when one person hurts another emotionally or physically: "See how it feels? This is how it feels!" Motives underlying rage and a desire for vengeance can combine with a need to be understood ("I want to hurt you, and I want you to hurt and feel my pain ... This is how it feels to be hurt!"). These actions may be triggered by being wounded somehow and a need to have the other person feel and understand those feelings, to empathize and do something about the situation. This dynamic is also seen in groups—group protests, riots, insurrections, strikes, revolts, and so on.

Empathy: Additional Questions

Many issues surrounding empathy still appear unsettled.

- **Is empathy innate?** I know of families with several children, one of whom seemed from the beginning to be more naturally empathic than the others.
- **Is empathy part of development?** Recall Alison Gopnik's cognitive studies of infants. She found that 18-month-olds had the capacity to understand that the experimenter liked the broccoli even when the babies did not . . . but that the 14-month-olds could not make that distinction. In contrast, Basch suggested that decentering, which is what Gopnik observed in an 18-month-old, was a necessary developmental step toward empathy that occurs much later—around Piaget's concrete operational stage, at about 7–11 years old.
- **Can empathy be developed or enhanced through therapy?** There is much to suggest that this occurs frequently (e.g., Basch, 1988). Much of therapy involves identifying with and learning from therapists' efforts to understand the internal world of other people. Various therapeutic theories (e.g., mentalization, mindfulness) have focused on the process of helping patients to develop the capacity for empathy, resulting in success in various modes of functioning (Fonagy et al., 2002; Hoffman et al., 2016).

Four Clinical Cases

Clinical treatment strategies put varying degrees of emphasis on aspects of affect, cognition, and language. Clinical work tends to utilize awareness of the therapist's own internal world, the patient's internal world, and various aspects of the external world. The following examples are presented briefly to illustrate a few ideas about these therapeutic processes, especially as related to the integration of affects, cognition, and language.

The four cases that follow are examples of child analysis, i.e., the child is seen by the therapist three to five times per week, and the parents are seen about every two to four weeks. Child analysis has tended to be conceptualized classically in terms of clinical theory and technique: establishing a relationship, an atmosphere of safety, and a developmental space within which to play; interpreting defense and resistance, anxiety and conflict, and unconscious fantasy; working with parents; and using one's countertransferences and analyzing the transferences (Yanof, 1996; Hoffman, 2007; Sugarman, 2009; Tyson, 2009).

However, discussions and cases have emerged in the literature suggesting that with more troubled children, some expansion of child analytic techniques may be more productive (Fonagy & Target, 1996b; Yanof, 1996; Tyson, 2009). This seems

Integrating Affects, Cognition, and Language 101

fueled particularly in the areas of affect and development (Greenspan, 1997; Hurry, 1998; Fonagy & Target, 1999; Holinger, 2016). The following cases are discussed in more detail elsewhere: Jeremy (Yanof, 1996); Peter (Tyson, 2009); Mark and David (Holinger, 2016).

Jeremy

By way of introduction, I will start with a brief description of a case presented by Judy Yanof, a child/adolescent psychoanalyst from Boston (1996). Jeremy was a four-and-a-half-year-old boy who was brought to Dr. Yanof because he wouldn't speak—he had selective mutism since he was about three years old. *Selective mutism* is a condition in which children stop speaking to nearly all but their closest family members, with whom they usually speak normally.

Jeremy was the oldest of three siblings, having two younger sisters. His parents were well-educated, engaging, and concerned about Jeremy. He was bright, active, and talked in sentences at about 20 months. He had temper tantrums from 18 months on, and his mother later noted that she thought he was spoiled—rather than seeing he was distressed and unhappy. Mother tried to make him comply; he fought her; she felt helpless; and she often became physical in trying to gain some control. Jeremy's first sister, Heather, was born when he was two. He was very jealous, even trying to fit into her baby clothes, and later he would attack her verbally and physically. He was scared of the dark, and he had frequent nightmares.

When he was a little over three years old, he entered preschool, and initially he did well. He became attached to Brita, a teacher who was six months pregnant. Three months later, Brita left to have her baby, and Jeremy's response was total

Photo 11.2 Judy Yanof
Source: Courtesy of Judy Yanof

silence. He stopped talking at school and became isolated. He talked at home, and when asked why he didn't talk at school, he said, "Because I have a magic mouth" (Yanof, 1996, p. 84).

Initially, Yanof was impressed with Jeremy's efforts to communicate nonverbally through gestures and drawings. Soon, however, he became unresponsive to her overtures for contact. Yanof noted, "I had to find a way to communicate with Jeremy without words since he rendered my words meaningless" (1996, p. 85). As she struggled to be attuned to and communicate with Jeremy, Yanof said she made a pivotal intervention:

> I began to speak to Jeremy in another language. I made noises . . . I became the soundtrack to Jeremy's play: a punch landed "POW," a guy fell "THUD," a car collided "CRASH!"—a cacophony of violent sounds. I joined his play; I gave it voice. Within a few days Jeremy began to make noises too—at first tentatively and then more deliberately and with greater abandon. His play had become communicative. It was accompanied by a range of sounds that clearly expressed affect. A man laughed evilly; a woman screamed helplessly; a child voiced surprise; another expressed disgust, all without words. We now had a dialogue about important matters replete with affects. It was as if the spell of the magic mouth had been broken.
>
> (p. 85)

Yanof elaborated on the complicated nature of this process: "The very act of speaking becomes engaged in conflict . . . the child equates it to an act of aggression" (p. 80), and the child defends against this forbidden impulse by not speaking. Certainly, it appeared that Yanof linked the affects to noises and then to words. "Like the special dialogue between mother and infant, my intervention amplified affect" (pp. 85–86). She also brings us back to Anny Katan's thoughts about early verbalization of affects. "*This has a resonance with A. Katan's (1961) idea about the significance of the young child's capacity to name and verbalize affects as a first step in tolerating and mastering them*" (p. 89, emphasis added).

Yanof herself grappled with what allowed Jeremy to talk: "This is hard to know for sure," she said, but already in therapy, his increased freedom in expressing his destructive thoughts in noisy but wordless play was helping "to detoxify the danger of his thoughts" (p. 88). She survived his attacks and put the unspeakable into words: "My words helped him to know and organize that which had previously been unknowable" (p. 88). Discussion of the rest of this fascinating analysis is beyond the scope of the current work, but it is well worth reading (Yanof, 1996).

Others have also discussed these processes involving affects and verbalization in clinical work, e.g., Ferro and Meregnani (1994), Lecours and Bouchard (1997), Brinich and Gilmore (2002), and Gedo (2005). As Gedo noted: "An affect has to become symbolically encoded . . . the absence of such encoding constitutes alexithymia" (2005, p. 90). (*Alexithymia* involves having no words for emotions; it is a failure to recognize one's own affects.) Gedo also noted that "the inability to encode certain matters verbally has profound adaptive disadvantages" (p. 109).

I turn now to another case that deals with the integration of affect, cognition, and language.

Mark

Mark was about four-and-a-half years old when I first met him. His analysis lasted approximately two-and-a-half years. Mark had been doing well until about nine months prior when a favorite sitter left for another job and his mother's outside work hours expanded. Mark had increasing difficulty at his preschool: He stopped talking and became virtually mute outside of his home; he began losing bowel and bladder control at school, had episodes of being inconsolable, and finally was asked to leave. He began to have periods of hyperventilation and did not want to leave his house; small cuts would require attention, many bandages, and temporary disuse of whatever limb was involved. He reacted fearfully to a rather violent TV commercial, and when it came on the screen, he would run away into another room. In addition, he began worrying about the police, fearing being arrested, and wondering whether the police could hear what he was thinking or saying. He would tap on the wall or a table and ask his mother, "Can the police hear that?"

Mark settled in quietly to the analysis over the first several months. He often included me in his play but responded only infrequently and briefly to any verbal interpretations I might make. Gradually, however, he began to be more mobile and less inhibited in his play. He found a ball and used it to play football. He would pretend to be a runner, struggling over tacklers and straining for the goal line. My efforts to talk with him about any of this, including how scary it was to talk at all, tended, for the most part, to be met with silence. I began to try to attune myself to his feelings by linking his bodily motions and play to noises with affectively laden words (Yanof, 1996; Stern, 1985). "Pow," "crunch," "smash," I would call out as he hit one tackler after another. He strained for the goal line. "Uhh . . . uhhh!" I groaned. He became more open with his own noises and facial expressions, especially around the goal line. He would growl and look angry and very frustrated as he tried but couldn't make it over the goal line.

I then began to try to interpret his feelings verbally and explicitly. "He is distressed . . . he is *mad*!" I called out. "He is so angry; he wants to get a touchdown!" As the play continued over the days and weeks, I said more: "Perhaps it's scary to feel and say these things." I also tried to address possible unconscious conflicts and fantasies: "You seem to want to score, but you're holding yourself back," or "What makes it so tough to score?" or "Maybe it scares you to score and win" or "Perhaps you are worried I'll be angry with you if you let yourself go and score and win."

Although it is difficult to know what was most useful, Mark became increasingly animated and verbal in his play. He began scoring touchdowns. He would cheer and celebrate, and I would join him, again interpreting his feelings: "He is excited, elated! He scores! He is celebrating!" At times, he would have me be the referee, and now he would be able to be angry at me directly: He would glare and growl at me, talking a bit more, sometimes getting in my face and saying, "I am mad!"

I became the announcer, who told of his feelings, or the interviewer, who would ask him after the game how he felt. He began to talk more about his feelings: "I feel great; we scored, we won!" Or "I am mad! I am angry (growl)! I hate the referee. And I don't like you either!" Now Mark was becoming more verbal, and his parents described significant changes occurring in his external world. He was back in preschool and doing well, talking and playing; the parents also mentioned that his symptoms at home had lessened significantly.

The next year and a half were marked by an interest I had heard about during the first few hours: wrestling. For the next year or so, Mark and I became immersed in a wrestling motif. He talked about the World Wrestling Federation (WWF), what he had seen on TV, the wrestlers themselves (Triple H., the Undertaker, Stone Cold Steve Austin, and many more), and the different kinds of matches. He would sometimes be one of the wrestlers and would take a pillow (the opponent) and pound it, throw it around, pin it, win, and raise his hands exultantly. At times, I was the announcer, calling out as he walked into the ring: "And now, at 39 pounds, the Undertaker!" and the crowd would go wild. Other times, I was the referee or the mean authoritative commissioner, often glared and growled at and argued with.

Gradually, board games began to dominate our sessions: checkers, chess, and Parcheesi. There was increased verbalization of the feelings, processes, and transferences involved, including his fear of playing up to his full potential. The work with the parents was rather straightforward, and I discussed the idea of innate affects with them, highlighting the various feelings Mark was expressing through his behaviors. We worked to understand further their son, as well as their own dynamics, feelings, and relationship.

This led toward termination. Mark was doing very well in school now, had friends, and was very involved in outside activities. He began to wonder about stopping, and ultimately, we set a termination date for several months in the future. He talked about how he would miss coming and miss me but how he was having fun with his friends. He would come back, he said, if he needed to, but the reasons he came in were becoming a little vague to him. The parents went through some mourning around the ending, and the mother became tearful as she talked about where her son had been when he first came in and where he was now.

Over the next few years, I occasionally heard from Mark and his parents. Later, when he was about 11 years old, I heard again from his mother. She said things were going well. Mark was getting into sports, especially basketball. His role was to run the team as point guard when he was on the court. "How do you do that," she asked him, "with the crowd noise and dealing with everything that's going on around you? How do you stay so calm and collected?" And now Mark (Mark who would not talk and was terrified of a TV commercial and being arrested) answered his mother with a statement and a question. "It seems easy, Mom," Mark said. "What's the big deal?"

The family and Mark have stayed in touch with me over the years. Initially, he became involved in security and police work. Then, in the midst of writing this chapter, I heard from his parents that Mark (now in his mid-20s) was excited about his new job as a firefighter in a large US city.

There are many theoretical and technique issues I might discuss (Holinger, 2016), but my major goals here involve giving examples of affect, cognition, and language as they interact with patients and parents in the clinical setting in early development. With Mark, my initial efforts to interpret his resistance and unconscious fantasies around talking seemed rather ineffective, so I began linking affectively laden words to Mark's play: Oomph! Bang! Crash! This was consistent with affect attunement in Stern's model of development in which issues of validation and sharing of affect in the domains of core and intersubjective self occur well prior to verbal encoding (Stern, 1985; Holinger, 1999); it was also similar to what Yanof and Katan described.

Very soon, I began interpreting the feelings related to these actions and noises: his distress, anger, fear, interest, and so on. This deepened the process in that his play intensified and morphed into the wrestling motif that was to characterize much of the analysis. Increasingly, he expressed his rage in his play as well as directly and verbally at me in the transference. Now, my comments about his reluctance to talk about his anger and his hesitation in winning led to his discussing both his fear and desire to hurt others and his apprehension of being retaliated against. We were able to talk openly about his fear of his own rage and aggressivity and his ambivalence toward me and his mother. With this transference work came other changes: Mark was able to think and talk more metaphorically, his play shifted, and his interests and ambitions began to emerge more clearly. This then launched into the termination phase of the analysis.

The next two examples show a rather different presentation—more chaotic and impulsive.

Peter

Phyllis Tyson, a child and adolescent psychoanalyst from California, described the beginning of the analysis of a very troubled eight-year-old boy named Peter.

> I was most puzzled by his total lack of . . . psychological mindedness. He did not seem to have any sense of who he was or what kind of emotional state he was in. He had no words for feelings, no capacity to think about and reflect on the feelings that might be causing some of his distress . . . Peter also had no tools with which to think about and reflect on the possible feelings of another person.
> (2009, pp. 934–935)

Peter's troubles seemed to begin early. His mother said she had difficulty comforting him and calming his incessant crying. Less than two years later, a baby sister was born, and Peter began to have sleep problems, exaggerated temper tantrums, and phobias. He also heard voices coming from the pipes in the house. When he turned three years old, Peter began to have nightmares. His behavior deteriorated, and his phobias increased. He was afraid to go upstairs alone, and he would take three or four hours to go to sleep. Peter was referred to the Anna Freud Centre for treatment, and he began five-times-weekly analysis a few months before he turned eight years old.

Photo 11.3 Phyllis Tyson
Source: Courtesy of Phyllis Tyson

As Dr. Tyson began working with Peter, she became aware of various problems with the treatment. Reflecting on these issues in her clinical technique, she noted: "I quickly realized that interpretations of unconscious conflict aimed at promoting insight were not helpful and did not lead to elaboration or the introduction of new material" (2009, p. 935). She then articulated the shifts she made.

> The strategy I developed in treating him was to focus on verbalizing his feelings and mental states, using Katan's notion (1961, p. 185) that verbalization of affect leads to some measure of control. She maintained that such verbalization increases ego strength by enabling the individual to distinguish between wishes and fantasies on the one hand, and reality on the other. I hoped that if I could consistently label Peter's feelings, and make links to his actions and subsequent feelings, he might, in time, be able himself to label and think about his mental states. My goal was to enable Peter to feel that he could control his feelings instead of his feelings controlling him.
>
> (p. 935)

For example, one day during a session, another patient barged into the room. Peter absolutely froze, and after she was escorted from the room, he resumed as if nothing had happened.

> After a while I commented on how frightened he looked when she barged in but that now he was pretending nothing had happened. He said he had felt "red" inside. We came to understand that the color red, for him, was the way he represented his anger. He also described how his head had spun around. He was not sure where he was, and he felt as if he were floating . . . and was afraid that first his brain, and then his mind, would explode.
>
> (p. 925)

Later in treatment, after much work on understanding his feelings and putting words to them, Tyson took time off for vacation. When she returned, Peter was withdrawn and angry. However, soon, he was able to talk about his sadness, disappointment, and anger—and then was able to articulate both his caring for and rage at Tyson—a deepening of his understanding of ambivalence.

The analysis wrapped up after about three years. At the end of treatment, Peter was functioning at home, socially, and at school. His temper tantrums and outbursts of anger were rare and manageable, and the phobias and nightmares were gone. As Tyson put it:

> He could also now think about and put words to his feelings and in doing so no longer felt like a volcano ready to explode . . . he was increasingly engaged with schoolwork and with friends . . . Developmentally, he was back on track.
>
> (p. 931)

A more detailed discussion of the analysis is beyond my scope here, but has been described in further depth by Tyson (2009).

In addition, follow-up interviews with Peter were conducted by researchers about 25 years after termination when Peter was in his 30s. Peter had become a computer software engineer. Tyson wrote about the follow-up:

> With Peter, labeling and exploring his 'red inside' and scary exploding earth-sun feelings gave them content and context and allowed him some mastery . . . The feeling that he has acquired some tools for mastery seems to have stayed with Peter and helped him through some of the more difficult parts of his life.
>
> (p. 941)

Peter himself commented during the follow-up on his current work and life: "Not perfect, but good enough . . . fixing bugs and making things work better" (p. 919).

David

David was about five years old when I first met him. This handsome little boy was brought to see me because he was about to get expelled from Junior Kindergarten. He was often out of control in the classroom, sometimes pushing or hitting other children, having tantrums, or sitting in an isolated fashion, not participating, and not responding. At home, he was volatile, angry, and often quite aggressive toward his younger siblings. His parents were very committed to him and motivated to help, and we began a four-times-per-week analysis. The first few months of the analysis saw frenetic activity in the sessions, with some calming as time went on. I worked to stay attuned to him as he went from one thing to another, and I actively interpreted his feelings as they emerged—his distress, excitement, rage, and so on. He tended not to respond to my efforts to explore his anxieties and fantasies. Some of the anger I had heard about was directed at me in the office.

The pivotal shift occurred about four months into treatment when David discovered I had a television in my office. He began to turn it on during the sessions, and he got intrigued with the cartoons. Soon, we pulled up chairs and watched TV together during the sessions. At that point, my feelings were quite mixed. What was going on? What did it mean? On the one hand, it seemed as if David had finally found an oasis in his world, a chance for quiet in the midst of a noisy household of siblings and parents. And something intrigued him—he was "playing" in his own way. On the other hand, I was horrified—watching television during sessions? But something was happening. We watched *Arthur, Clifford, George Shrinks, Transformers, Berenstain Bears*, and others. I tended to comment on what was happening and interpreted the feelings of the characters. They became our friends.

One day, we were watching *George Shrinks* together. George is a little boy, around ten years old; he is about three inches tall and lives with a normal-sized family. He is quite amicable and capable, having his own airplane/car/boat-submarine that he uses adeptly. At one point, George inadvertently gets wrapped up inside a box and mailed overseas. His mother becomes distraught. Stunningly, David turned to me, his eyes wide, and said: "His mother misses him!" We talked about this, how his mother felt, how scared and lost and alone George felt. The door began to open. As time went on, I took David's lead and started more explicitly to interpret the affects the characters were conveying: their distress, anger, shame, and excitement. David joined in, commenting about their feelings and actions.

The work with the parents continued: We talked about David's fears and anger in various situations. Discussing these issues using specific affects seemed to help the parents gain a sense of David's internal world, with his own feelings and interests that motivated his behavior. As they became increasingly able to give voice to their own feelings about their son, they were able to create an atmosphere in which David was more and more comfortable speaking to them about his feelings, especially his anger. The parents were then able to use these words with David, which he picked up on.

In David's external world, things were changing dramatically. He was doing very well in school, both behaviorally and intellectually. There was no more discussion about him being asked to leave the school, and his teachers seemed to like him a great deal. He had friends now, and play dates went well.

As David approached seven years of age and after about two years of analysis, we began to consider termination. One day, shortly before termination, I was meeting with the parents, and the father said he had an incident to tell me about. "There had been a kind of noisy family fight, and afterward, I couldn't find David," the father started out. "I finally found him on the front steps. 'David,' I said, 'what's going on?' And David said to me, 'Daddy, I was very angry at you . . . and I didn't know if I wanted to talk with you directly about it yet or come out here and calm myself down and think about it first.'"

The use of the television, cartoons, and movies by David and other children deserves further discussion. Initially, I was quite apprehensive as David was drawn to the television and the various cartoons with which he was familiar. Yet, as Judy Yanof noted, this is the world most of these children live in these days—television, cartoons, video games, and movies (personal communication).

Subsequently, I have worked with several children who gravitated to those venues during periods of their treatment. Developmentally, most of them were in latency. One consistent feature seems to be the affective resonance between the characters in the television or movies and the patient's internal experience. The facial expressions, the behaviors, the words, and the verbal volume and intonations are all part of the affective exchange.

To my surprise, a show with which I initially had very little familiarity seemed to be quite beneficial to some children—*The Simpsons*. The explicit and intense expression of affect in this show appeared to be true to life and allowed for discussion of the patients' own feelings and those of their parents and siblings. In a couple of instances of significant pathological inhibition, the lack of verbal and behavioral inhibition in *The Simpsons* seemed to provide an effective springboard for interpreting the fear, anger, and excitement of these children. Parents were often skeptical, but the children's occasional use of these venues provided another opportunity to discuss with the parents how child analysis, work in displacement, and focus on affects can lead to change.

Consistent with these ideas is the use of videos in psychotherapy training—that is, pictures as well as words can be helpful. Some have found that videos of therapy sessions, which are then viewed together by the patient and therapist, can be quite useful (e.g., Bhaskar Sripada, personal communication).

The Impact of Words: Feelings, Actions, and Interpersonal Skills

This discussion suggests the importance of linking feelings, cognition, and words in the context of development, empathy, and clinical work. This process has benefits in enhancing tension-regulation and self-soothing, promoting verbalization, and increasing thoughtfulness and goals rather than impulsive action.

Verbalizing—using words—is also an action. Words can have an impact. Enhanced self-awareness is useful—the internal freedom to have whatever thoughts and feelings come to our mind, to be playful with our various feelings and fantasies inside of ourselves. This awareness permits greater control over our actions and behavior—including our words. We have a better chance of controlling our behaviors if we are aware of our feelings and what is motivating us.

In terms of interpersonal skills, it can be beneficial to appreciate that our words are actions. We can hurt or heal with words. So, while at the same time promoting linking words with feelings, we also need to be aware of the impact of the words and verbalizing on others. Aristotle's words bear repeating: "Anyone can become angry—that is easy. But to be angry with the right person, to the right degree, at the right time, for the right purpose, and in the right way—that's not easy" (2002).

Up to this point in the book, the major focus has been on early development, individuals, and their parents and environment. There are also important societal implications of this work, and it is to those that we now turn.

Part 2

Societal Implications of Understanding Affects, Cognition, and Language

Views on Overcoming Physical Punishment and Bias, Prejudice, and Violence

Introduction to Part 2
Physical Punishment and Toward Understanding Bias, Prejudice, and Violence

I have long wanted to explore parallels between early developmental issues and larger societal concerns. My longstanding interest in the dynamics between individuals and groups took firm hold during the 1970s and 1980s. (This was in Chicago at the Psychosomatic and Psychiatric Institute [P&PI], with Roy R. Grinker, Sr., MD, and Daniel Offer, MD, and in Boston at the Harvard University School of Public Health, with Jane Murphy, PhD.) A group of us explored the epidemiology (prevalence and distribution of disease) of violent deaths in the US—suicide, homicide (those killed), and accidents.

Among other results, we found that over the prior 50 years (1933–1982), the death rates of suicide, homicide, and accidents all tended to increase and decrease in tandem. In addition, these changes in rates over time appeared related to periods of social change, for instance, economic depressions, wars, and population shifts (Holinger, 1987; Holinger et al., 1987). In this book, I was interested to see if it might be useful to explore various social problems via early development and the lenses of affect, cognition, and language.

Initially, I considered four social issues: physical punishment and violence; bias and prejudice; religious extremism; and education. Yet, in examining these further, I began to wonder if many of the dynamics underlying these social issues were all of a piece and had much to do with the areas that provide a focus for this book: affects, cognition, and language. In addition, violence is a frequent outcome of all four—physical punishment, bias and prejudice, religious extremism, and educational failings. So, I decided to narrow the chapters down to two social issues: physical punishment and bias, prejudice, and violence. Religious extremism will be included in bias and prejudice, and education is addressed briefly at several points in Chapters 8, 12, and 13.

These topics will be presented from both individual and social perspectives, that is, from the bottom up and top down—using individual data to understand groups better and vice versa. They will be explored through the lenses of affects, cognition, and language. A few of the questions considered: How might affect theory enhance our knowledge of the roles of distress, fear, shame, and anger in prejudice, self-esteem issues, and violence? Might increased awareness of the flaws in cognitive processes and educational shortcomings be useful in distinguishing between

DOI: 10.4324/9780429203640-14

Photo P2.1 Chuck Strozier
Source: Photograph by Paul Dry

Photo P2.2 David Terman
Source: Courtesy of David Terman

scientific data and false information? And how might language and the importance of words help society deal with feelings and cognition in such areas as physical punishment and prejudice?

Understanding the similarities and differences between individuals and groups has long been the subject of much work and controversy (e.g., Freud, 1921; Lewin, 1943; Grinker, 1956; Bion, 1959; Arendt, 1966; von Bertalanffy, 1968; Arato & Gebhardt, 1982; Kohut, 1985; Holinger, 1987; Lifton, 2000; Strozier et al., 2010; Kernberg, 1975, 2020). Freud introduced his discussion of these issues in the following way:

> The contrast between individual psychology and social or group psychology, which at first glance may seem to be full of significance, loses a great deal of its sharpness when it is examined more closely. It is true that individual psychology is concerned with the individual man and explores the paths by which he seeks to find satisfaction for his instinctual impulses; but only rarely and under certain exceptional conditions is individual psychology in a position to disregard the relations of this individual to others. In the individual's mental life someone else is invariably involved, as a model, as an object, as a helper, as an opponent; and so from the very first individual psychology, in this extended but entirely justifiable sense of the words, is at the same time social psychology as well.
>
> (1921, p. 69)

One of the most interesting current discussions of the complex interactions between individuals and groups is found in *The Fundamentalist Mindset: Psychological Perspectives on Religion, Violence, and History* (Strozier et al., 2010), and particularly in the two papers by David Terman, "Theories of Group Psychology, Paranoia, and Rage" and "Fundamentalism and the Paranoid Gestalt." Terman notes that "the group is not the individual writ large" (p. 16); the organization and goals of the group are not necessarily the same as the individuals. One of the important differences between individuals and groups is the loss of restraint in those caught up in the excitement and rage of mob action: Individuals commit violent acts that they would not do if they were alone.

However, Terman continues,

> Though the individual and the group are not synonymous, each profoundly affects the other. For example, deeply held aspects of the individual self are invested in the group self, and it is evident that intense affects are generated in the individual when the group is perceived as threatened with extinction or humiliation.
>
> (p. 17)

Terman then uses self-psychological concepts to suggest that

> one possible bridging concept between the individual and the group is the 'group self' that Heinz Kohut described . . . Like an individual, the group organizes itself with core ambitions and ideals, and these account for the sense of continuity and cohesion of the group.
>
> (p. 21)

The resulting sense of belonging in the group is an important element in the self-esteem, internal stability, and behavior of the individuals.

I am intrigued by the issues considered in this section, and I am particularly focused on actions and solutions. I hope that by exploring human development in the context of affect, cognition, and language, new and useful ideas may emerge about how we can understand and defuse the harm done by individual dynamics and social and cultural attitudes that motivate physical punishment, bias, prejudice, and the associated violence.

Chapter 12

Physical Punishment
"The Canary in the Coal Mine"

Chapter Outline:

- Defining physical punishment
- Factors that contribute to the use of physical punishment
- The impact of physical punishment
- Physical punishment—Individuals
- Physical punishment—Society
- International trends
- Potential solutions and prevention of physical punishment—Individuals
- Potential solutions and prevention of physical punishment—Society
- Summarizing

With the following quote, Tomkins powerfully introduces the topic of physical punishment and the problems caused by the affect of anger when dealing with children.

> The whole spectrum of psychopathology is intimately linked with punitive socialization of anger . . . There is no affect whose punitive socialization can more jeopardize human development.
>
> (1991, p. 225)

Physical punishment is like the canary in the coal mine. It is a signal of impending danger. It is a wake-up call, alerting us to take early development seriously, to understand how feelings work, and to be aware of the variables that contribute to violence.

It was a strange feeling: as I went over this material, I realized that even as a youngster, I never understood physical punishment—the violence, impulsivity, lack of thoughtfulness, and tension regulation—whether at friends' houses, school, my household (relatively little), the playgrounds. The notion that physical punishment—with its hurt, rage, and shame—was a helpful thing to do in raising children seemed so absurd. It was a feeling of "how bizarre is this . . . it makes no sense."

DOI: 10.4324/9780429203640-15

Yet, as I grew older, I seemed at least to understand better *why* it happens. Often, it results from parents' efforts to change behaviors and protect the child, and it is an expression of overwhelming distress in the parent, leading to rage and violence. It is clearly a situation in which the three information processing systems of affects, cognition, and language fail us. The negative affects can be overpowering; cognition at times is inadequate to lead to changes in affect management or to support self-reflection and restraint; and language becomes more inflammatory than helpful.

I sometimes call physical punishment "the other plague." In some ways, it is as deadly, or even more so, than COVID-19.

- Physical punishment is damaging psychologically and physically.
- It is prevalent in approximately 50 to 60 percent of US households with children.
- It is frequently transmitted from generation to generation.
- The sequelae are many and severe (e.g., violence, drug abuse, delinquency, domestic violence, and child abuse).

Physical punishment has long been a persistent human behavior—a behavior that people have been profoundly reluctant to abandon or even modify (Straus et al., 2014; Holden, 2020; Holinger, 2020).

In this exploration of physical punishment, I will first define physical punishment and then provide a brief synthesis of the variables that contribute to it. Next, I look at physical punishment via affects, cognition, and language in both individuals and society in order to provide further understanding of their use and misuse

Photo 12.1 Elizabeth Gershoff

Source: This file is licensed under the Creative Commons Attribution-Share Alike 4.0 International license

and the resulting psychopathology. Then, I will discuss the international trends in the acceptance and rejection of physical punishment. And finally, I will attempt to integrate these ideas into a series of potential solutions.

Defining Physical Punishment

Traditionally, *physical punishment* has been defined as "the use of physical force with the intention of causing a child to experience bodily pain or discomfort, so as to correct or punish the child's behavior" (Gershoff, 2008, p. 9). Behaviors that cause physical injury are termed *physical abuse*. Physical punishment can be inflicted via spanking, shaking, hitting, pinching, squeezing, paddling, whippings, whupping, swatting, smacking, slapping, washing a child's mouth out with soap, making a child kneel on painful objects, and forcing a child to stand or sit in painful positions for long periods of time. As noted by the National Clearinghouse on Child Abuse and Neglect, physical abuse involves "the infliction of physical injury as a result of punching, beating, kicking, biting, burning, shaking, or otherwise harming a child" (Gershoff, 2002, p. 540).

However, physical punishment can be as damaging to children's healthy development as physical abuse, and most recent research questions the traditional physical punishment-abuse dichotomy: Physical abuse tends to occur during episodes of physical punishment (Fortson et al., 2016). Verbal abuse is also at issue here, as it can elicit the same development-damaging affects as physical punishment and abuse—e.g., distress, anger, fear, and shame—with denigration and disruption of self-development (e.g., Demos, 1989, 2019; Tomkins, 1992).

The terms *corporal punishment* and *spanking* tend to obscure the understanding of the impact of physical punishment. Many people do not know that *corporal* means of the body or physical. *Spanking* is a euphemism for hitting. One is not permitted to hit one's spouse or a stranger; such actions are defined as the crime of battery.

The puzzle and persistence of physical punishment are not simply abstract issues: Profound individual psychopathology and social problems are indisputably associated with physical punishment. It is to these issues that we turn now.

Factors That Contribute to the Use of Physical Punishment

The reasons that adults inflict physical and emotional harm on children are complex. Holden (2020) noted the wide range of categories associated with physical punishment. He divided the data into *sociocultural determinants* (e.g., social norms where parents reside); *family social environment determinants* (such as family structure, marital relationship, and stress); *child determinants* (age, sex, behavior, temperament, presence of a disability); and *parental determinants* (age, childhood history, mental health, conscious thoughts, and unconscious motives).

Using these categories, Holden makes it possible to highlight many conditions and affects in individuals and situations that contribute to the infliction of physical punishment, for example, frustration, exhaustion, fear, and rage of a stressed parent or caregiver; one's own upbringing, identification with the aggressor, and intergenerational psychopathology (the bullied become bullies); blaming (externalizing processes) (Hoffman & Prout, 2020); compromised socioeconomic status (SES); less education; certain religious beliefs (Holden, 2020); erotic aspects, for both the perpetrator and the victim (Rousseau, 1782/1945; Cranston, 1982); and masochism and sadism (Novick & Novick, 2020).

The Impact of Physical Punishment

Hitting a child elicits precisely the negative affects a parent, caretaker, or other abuser does not want to generate in a child: distress, anger, fear, shame, disgust, and dissmell. Studies show that children who are hit identify with the aggressor and are more likely to become hitters themselves, that is, bullies and future abusers of their own children and partners. They tend to learn to use violent behavior as a way to deal with stress and interpersonal disputes.

A massive body of literature on physical punishment has emerged over the past several decades. As George Holden noted:

> In the case of hitting a child—commonly and euphemistically called corporal punishment (CP)—there is now a very large corpus of studies, numbering well over 1,500 empirical investigations, that have established that this behavior is linked to a variety of negative outcomes in children. The problems included a vast spectrum of behavioral, relationship, and emotional difficulties, as well as physical child abuse.
> (2020, p. 10)

It is beyond my scope here to review this literature in detail. Among the most recent and complete reviews are Straus et al., 2014; Gershoff & Grogan-Kaylor, 2016; Durrant & Ensom, 2017; Holden, 2020; Heilmann et al., 2021; and *The Psychoanalytic Study of the Child*, which devoted an entire section to the "Problem of Physical Punishment and Its Persistence" (2020, Volume 73: 1–108).

With regard to the impact of physical punishment, perhaps the best summary is that of Murray Straus, Emily Douglas, and Roseanne Medeiros in *The Primordial Violence: Spanking Children, Psychological Development, Violence, and Crime* (2014). They summarized 15 harmful effects associated with physical punishment found by their reviews and research:

- More antisocial behavior and delinquency as a child and as a young adult
- More approval of other forms of violence

Photo 12.2 Murray A. Straus

Source: Photograph courtesy of Emily M. Douglas, PhD

- More impulsiveness and less self-control
- Worse parent-child relationships
- More risky sexual behaviors as a teenager
- More juvenile delinquency
- More crime perpetrated as an adult
- Lower national average mental ability
- Less probability of graduation from college
- High probability of depression
- More violence against marital, cohabitating, and dating partners
- More violence against nonfamily persons
- More physical abuse of children
- More drug abuse
- More sexual coercion and physically forced sex

In addition, recent neurobiological research suggests that physical punishment may affect the brain development of children (e.g., Cuartas et al., 2021).

Furthermore, as a remarkable study by Holden and his colleagues shows, the problem may be worse than we think (2014). Most studies of physical punishment are self-reports. Holden and his groups, using recorders (with the subjects' knowledge and permission) in addition to self-reports, documented that physical punishment occurred at least five times as much as reported via self-reporting measures.

Photo 12.3 George Holden
Source: Courtesy of George Holden

Physical Punishment—Individuals

The three information processing systems, which have been the focus of this book, can enhance our understanding of the impact of physical punishment on individuals and on the social fabric. Let's first take a look at the interaction of physical punishment and affects as it plays out in individuals—victims as well as caregivers—and then turn to society.

Affects

As discussed in Chapters 2 and 3, negative affects are SOS signals. Excessive triggering of any negative affect can lead to distress and then anger. This is "stress," "too muchness." So, what happens in physical punishment?

Physical punishment can elicit and solidify in the child precisely the affects the parent or caregiver does not want to take center stage with respect to development, e.g., distress, anger, fear, shame, disgust, and dissmell.

In the midst of multiple motives, there may be unconscious identifications with the aggressor, unconscious aggression or sadism toward the baby, and an unconscious parental transference toward the child (see the discussion of Winnicott later in this section). Children may identify with the actions and affects of their caregivers and internalize them—the rage and the violence. These negative affects and behaviors can then impair the children's character structure, putting them at risk of becoming a bully, even as youngsters, and then passing the behavioral patterns that result from the negative affects on to their own children (Durrant & Ensom, 2012; Straus et al., 2014; Gershoff & Grogan-Kaylor, 2016; Holden, 2020).

As Claudia Lament noted, there is tremendous unconscious power in identification with the aggressor, whether that is an abusive parent of the past, authority figures, or whomever. The experience of turning prior feelings of helplessness from childhood into becoming the sadistic master of the child may take over. For the abusive parent in the present, their own parent of yore may be embedded in the child who is being beaten (personal communication).

How about those who inflict physical punishment? The caregivers are often stressed out, angry, and scared. They may be fearful of being seen as bad parents whose child is poorly behaved, or perhaps their child has done or said something provocative or stirred up some difficult feelings from the parent's own childhood.

And there are other reasons in a parent or caregiver for the anger underlying physical punishment. There is a love-hate ambivalence in human relationships, conscious or unconscious. That is, positive and negative affects are both involved in the most loving relationships, even in the mother-infant bond. Donald Winnicott, MD, pointed this out dramatically in his iconic paper "Hate in the Counter-Transference" (1949). "We know about a mother's love and we appreciate its reality and power. Let me give some of the reasons why a mother hates her baby" (p. 73). Winnicott then lists 18 reasons why a mother may sometimes hate her baby. I will paraphrase a few of these.

- The baby is a danger to her body in pregnancy and at birth.
- The baby is an interference with her private life, a challenge to preoccupation.
- To a greater or lesser extent, a mother feels that her own mother demands a baby so that her baby is produced to placate her mother.
- The baby hurts her nipples even by suckling, which is, at first, a chewing activity.
- The baby is ruthless, treats her as scum, an unpaid servant, a slave.
- At first, the baby does not know at all what the mother does or what she sacrifices for him.

This paper was followed by other works that highlighted the aggression as well as the love that is felt simultaneously in parenting (e.g., Beiser, 1989; Rosenblitt, 2009; Young-Bruehl, 2012). Thus, the parent-child bond is loaded with intense affect, both positive and negative.

There are two other factors that add to the mix: contagion and fear.

First, as discussed in Chapter 7, anger and other negative affects can be contagious. Excessive negative affects in either parent or child can lead to a contagious reaction, in which one reaction or remark by the child or parent leads to another in one or both of them. As that bounces back and forth between child and parent, it can escalate, and soon hitting and violence can ensue, the result of the contagion of negative affects. At the same time, positive affects may be impaired, such as enjoyment in the relationship. Perhaps most importantly, when this maelstrom of emotions erupts between parent and child, the capacity of both for interest (curiosity) can be compromised. Even after the incident is over, it may be difficult for either to be curious about what triggered the words or actions.

Second, the other factor involves the affects of surprise, fear, and interest. Recall that any stimulus with a relatively sudden onset in the rate of neural firing will innately trigger surprise or startle; if the rate increases less rapidly, fear and terror are elicited; and if still less rapidly, interest and excitement occur, as the brain begins to process the stimulus. As discussed in Chapter 3, both the nature of the external stimulus and the child's temperament and experience are taken into account and combined to determine the density of neural firing. The result may be more fear-laden or a more rapid transition to interest.

The important issue here is the infant or young child's otherness—*differentness*—from the adult. The infant and young child don't look like, behave, or communicate like the adult parent. They may startle, scare, enrage, or delight the adult, depending, for instance, on the adult's temperament and how much understanding and experience the adult has with children. These differences may act as stimuli to the parent's fear and anger and impulse to use physical punishment, as the parent tries to socialize the child and help them develop.

The affect of interest and the capacity for empathy are keys to these challenges. The importance of responding with curiosity and empathy to differences will resonate throughout the later chapters of this book.

Cognition

In the midst of a squabble and excessive negative affects involving caregivers and children, what happens to cognition? How does the squabble play out? The caregiver's tension regulation may be compromised at the moment, and the frustration and anger are too much and overwhelm the cognitive capacities to think things through. The negative affects interfere with various aspects of cognition, e.g., thinking, problem-solving, and self-reflection. The parent is then less able to understand what has happened, sort things out, and find nonviolent solutions. The affects can overcome cognitive capacities and swamp any knowledge that physical punishment does more harm than good.

The child's cognitive processes are also impacted. The pain of the physical punishment, possibly combined with harsh words and noise, may impair the child's cognitive capacities to understand what has happened and what is being communicated. In addition, there is an overarching message with which the child may identify: Violence is a good way to solve problems.

Language

Language, too, becomes vulnerable. Anny Katan's work (1961) shows the power of putting words into feelings at an early age. But in a heated squabble, affects such as distress, anger, or fear may overwhelm both parent and child's capacity to employ words—words that could be used to calm the storm so that parent and child might work toward understanding what happened or even agreeing to disagree. Both perpetrator and victim may be acting and speaking before they think—they are not able to reflect, calm themselves, and use their cognition and curiosity to address the problem and carve out some solutions with words. The healthy use of language during conflict depends on the use of reasoned cognition.

A Brief Example

Say a four-year-old boy is lying on the floor with some crayons, markers, and paper while his father works nearby. The little boy begins drawing on the rug rather than on the paper. Dad ultimately sees this and gets angry, telling his son to draw on the paper, not on the rug. But soon, the boy starts on the rug again. Father swats him, and the boy howls and calls the father stupid or some such. Mother comes in at this point and says, "Don't talk to your father like that!" The negative affects are being mobilized by everyone—distress, anger, fear, and shame. More noise, tears. The contagion of the negative affects has been triggered. Mobilizing positive affects—e.g., curiosity—is no longer possible. Cognitive processes are not functioning well—what is happening here? What are the causes underneath the behavior? Rather than trying to use words to understand the feelings behind the actions, language just inflames matters. Silvan Tomkins commented on the power of anger in these situations: "The experience or the possibility of the feeling of anger can come to evoke utter humiliation or guilt, or anguish, or overwhelming terror" (1991, p. 225).

Alternative ways of dealing with these scenarios involve focusing on the positive aspects of affects, cognition, and language. For example, there is increasing evidence that focusing on the positive affects of interest and enjoyment is more effective than the negative affects in creating behavioral change (e.g., Holden, 2020; Durrant, 2016; Sege et al., 2018).

With the young child drawing on the rug, the parent might have better results by supporting his drawing in general rather than just criticizing the rug drawing. Or a parent might offer the information that, "Hmmm . . . we can't draw on the rug . . . If you draw on the paper, we can save your drawing and hang it on the wall! Would you do that so I can save your artwork?" Or empathize and say, "You really like to draw, don't you? I love that you do!" And even add, with a chuckle, "Well, thank you for not drawing on the wall, too!" This approach may well open the door to being curious about and understanding what feelings were possibly behind the rug drawing. Was the child simply not remembering that drawing had to stay on the paper? Or was it intriguing to see what kind of marks and colors would be made on the rug?

And, perhaps gradually, the parent could begin to put words to the feelings and work things out. In this scenario, positive aspects of affects, cognition, and language are mobilized via interest and empathy—with subsequent behavioral change and more successful socialization (for more examples of these processes, see Durrant, 2016; Holinger, 2003).

Physical Punishment—Society

On a larger public health level, how does the issue of physical punishment play out in society? Why doesn't the overall society and its many distinct cultures see the problems, damage, and violence that physical punishment creates? Much has been written about this blindness. For instance, the titles of three excellent summaries overtly ask this question: "Why Do Parents Hit Their Children? From Cultural to Unconscious Determinants" (Holden, 2020); "Why Won't They Learn: Unconscious Underpinnings of Corporal Punishment" (Novick & Novick, 2020); and "Why Can't We See It?" (Spira, 2020).

On the social level, there appears to be a lack of awareness of the problems associated with physical punishment. The data against physical punishment are compelling, but it seems as if social policymakers (as well as individuals) are either unaware of the information, dismiss it, or are unable to change it.

There appear to be a variety of reasons for the persistence of physical punishment in societies and our difficulty in bringing our collective cognitive capacities to bear on this problem. In some societies and cultures, there is a lack of dissemination of information and data about physical punishment, disavowal and denial of the harm caused by physical punishment, intergenerational pathology, identifying with aggressors and parents doing what was done to them, fear and shame of raising unsocialized and out-of-control children, and stunted interest (that is, decreased curiosity on the part of parents and children regarding feelings and behaviors).

Affects

Two issues are notable here with respect to the role of affect in physical punishment in society. The first is the notion of contagion; the second involves the affect of interest. Contagion is seen in the following manner, and it is somewhat different than in individuals. There is a sense in society that everyone uses some physical punishment; everyone does it—at least a little—so why not do it? In the United States, the incidence of physical punishment in families has been slowly decreasing over time, and yet it remains a way of imposing discipline in around 50 to 60 percent of families, generating the sense that it must be all right. There is no "voice of the law" telling people to stop and reflect on what they are doing.

This also relates to the second issue—the stifling on a broad societal scale of the affect of interest. In a society that endorses physical punishment, there is little to trigger the curiosity of people about their own (or their children's) behavior as they hit their children. There still appears not to be enough importance and publicity given to early development and the problem of physical punishment. Many adults live in a culture that blocks them from ever asking themselves: Why am I doing this? Is it working? Does it make things better or worse? What were my child's feelings that resulted in her actions? What are my feelings and my actions?

Cognition

Society fails to embrace the positive powers of cognition when it allows or encourages the perpetuation of physical punishment. This happens in part because of a widespread tendency for policymakers, teachers, social workers, physicians, and individuals to focus on behaviors rather than on causes and meanings that underlie behaviors (an important cognitive failure on the part of society and its members). We see this especially with society's "rules" about the socialization of children—rules that put a premium on behavior over understanding.

On the social level, there appears to be a lack of awareness (there's that muted cognition again) of the problems associated with physical punishment. The data against physical punishment are compelling, but it seems as if social policymakers (as well as individuals) are either unaware of the information, dismiss it, or are unable to change.

Language

The power of language is often overlooked, and the way social policies wield language (on paper and in laws) often distorts its meaning. The terms *spanking* and *a little swat* minimize the impact of the word *hitting*.

Laws prohibiting physical punishment have the capacity to bring attention to the damage caused by physical punishment and highlight the benefits of alternatives. Such laws in many countries are linked with programs to help parents and children. Just the existence of such laws can raise social awareness of the problem—the voice and language of the law. As discussed next, such laws have led to many areas of positive social changes.

International Trends

Social change takes time. Consider the initial resistance to using seatbelts, or responding to the health problems of smoking, or the entrenched problems of racial and ethnic discrimination. Fortunately, however, there does seem to be progress: Increasing awareness of the problem and the rule of law appear to be having a positive impact. Scientific data and social change have led to international efforts to prohibit physical punishment.

Internationally, there is increasing consensus that the physical punishment of children violates international human rights laws (Bitensky, 2006). The United Nations Convention on the Rights of the Child (CRC, or the Children's Convention, adopted in 1989) presents one of the most comprehensive cases regarding the prohibition of physical punishment of children. In an attempt to stop what is called "legalized violence" toward children, and in response to the emerging data, the United Nations proposed a ban on physical punishment of children in the CRC. By 1990, as scientific research began showing a strong relationship between physical punishment and negative developmental outcomes, four countries (Sweden, Finland, Norway, and Austria) had banned physical punishment in all settings.

Currently, 196 countries are party to the CRC, including every member of the United Nations, with the exception of the United States. In 2006, the CRC stated in General Comment No. 8 that "The Committee is issuing this general comment to highlight the obligation of all States parties to move quickly to prohibit and eliminate all corporal punishment and all other cruel or degrading forms of punishment of children" (Committee on the Rights of the Child, 2006, p. 3), and that all States must "take all appropriate legislative, administrative, social, and educational measures to protect the child from all forms of physical or mental violence, injury or abuse" (p. 6).

Such work has currently led to over 125 countries prohibiting physical punishment in schools and 64 countries banning physical punishment in all settings, including the home. Among the 64 are Sweden, Finland, France, Spain, Austria, Germany, Israel, Kenya, Tunisia, Venezuela, Argentina, and Brazil. The laws and consequences tend to be more educative (about parenting and development) than punitive.

Are there studies of outcomes in countries that have prohibited physical punishment? Joan Durrant is a global leader in studying and publicizing the trends in physical punishment throughout the world. She and her colleague Anne Smith co-edited a study titled *Global Pathways to Abolishing Physical Punishment: Realizing Children's Rights* (Durrant & Smith, 2011). To summarize, the findings suggested that countries that banned physical punishment tended to have less physical punishment of children, enhanced parent-child relationships, and less violence in the society. More recently, Karin Österman and her colleagues conducted studies more than 25 years after the complete ban on physical punishment in Finland in 1983 (2014, 2018). The results showed a continuous significant decline in self-reported physical punishment after the establishment of the law—and a similar decline in the number of murdered children. It was concluded that a shift in the mindset toward a culture of nonviolent childrearing can be observed in Finland.

Photo 12.4 Joan Durrant
Source: Courtesy of Joan Durrant

However, the legal issues involving physical punishment are not insignificant. As Clare Huntington notes, in the United States, two trends tend to inhibit further legal prohibition of physical punishment: the history of parental rights over children vs. state rights and the potential negative sequelae of state services taking over the children (Roberts, 2002; Huntington, 2014, 2020).

The American Academy of Pediatrics (AAP), the American Psychological Association (APA), the American Medical Association (AMA), the American Academy of Child and Adolescent Psychiatry (AACAP), and the American Psychiatric Association (APA) each recently issued new position statements opposing the use of physical punishment and urging alternatives. AAP's Robert Sege noted that physical punishment of children has three major deleterious consequences: increasing aggressive behavior and more problems with parents and in school, adverse effects on children's brain development, and increased mental health problems (Abbasi, 2019). All these organizations oppose physical punishment and urge the use of alternatives. These alternatives usually include some form of *verbalization* ("words instead of action") and *internalization* ("set a good example"). The American Psychological Association's Resolution on Physical Discipline of Children by Parents states:

> Physical discipline by parents has been associated with heightened risk for harm to children's mental health, as well as to their cognitive, behavioral, social and emotional development . . . Physical discipline is associated with increased adverse outcomes for children across racial, ethnic, and socioeconomic groups and across community contexts.
>
> (February, 2019)

However, at the time of this writing, none of these organizations have proposed a *prohibition* of physical punishment, often due to legal concerns about intrusion by the state as well as religious or cultural reasons of some members. This results in what Straus et al. (2014) call Paradox #3: Focusing Exclusively on Teaching "Alternatives" Results in Almost Everyone Spanking (p. 274).

In the United States, the Centers for Disease Control and Prevention (CDC, Atlanta, Georgia) has now formally come out with policies and legislative recommendations asserting that physical punishment is child abuse (p. 8) and that it should be prohibited (p. 46) (Fortson et al., 2016). The American Psychoanalytic Association (APsA Position Statement on Physical Punishment, 2021) and the Association for Child Psychoanalysis (ACP) have joined the CDC in calling for policies and legislation *prohibiting* physical punishment in all settings. This stance is in response to data consistently showing physical punishment to be associated with increased violence and psychopathology. The United States has no federal law prohibiting physical punishment. In addition, there are still 17 states that permit physical punishment in public schools.

In 2023, the Protecting our Students in Schools Act of 2023 was reintroduced in the US Congress, sponsored by Senator Chris Murphy, Congresswoman Suzanne Bonamici, and others. This bill would federally prohibit the practice of physical punishment in any school in the United States that receives federal funding.

Potential Solutions and Prevention of Physical Punishment—Individuals

How might a focus on affects, cognition, and language help to decrease physical punishment and increase nonviolent methods of behavioral change?

Affects

Focusing on the idea that feelings underlie behaviors can assist parents and caregivers to understand infancy and early development better. The result will be curiosity on the part of parents about their children's feelings and curiosity in children as they develop, helping cognition and empathy flourish. Enhancing curiosity (interest) will increase self-reflection and empathy in both caregivers and children.

Cognition

Nurturing cognition in individuals improves parent-child interactions. Children can recognize patterns much earlier and more readily than previously thought, and they will be responsive to parents' use of positive affects, the naming of feelings, and the use of common sense about why things should or shouldn't be allowed. In addition, increasing the information stream to the public about the problems associated with physical punishment can help decrease violence. Increased information helped decrease smoking, increase the use of seatbelts, and improve the response to COVID-19.

Language

Parents can benefit from appreciating that children can understand language far earlier than they previously thought—and that's why labeling the affects as soon as possible encourages healthy development. As shown by the work of Katan (1961) and others (Yanof, 1996; Tyson, 2009; Holinger, 2016), talking with children, asking questions, and paying attention to their opinions as expressed through feelings and behaviors is so important.

Specific Alternatives

The following solutions integrate affects, cognition, and language in a series of ideas about specific alternatives to physical punishment and what is useful in decreasing physical punishment and violence. Various psychological and medical associations have provided several evidence-based alternatives that help reduce physical punishment. These tend to fall into five categories: listening, talking, and discussing; labeling feelings; positive reinforcement; teaching by example; and parents and caregivers taking care of themselves (e.g., APsA Position Statement on Physical Punishment, 2021; American Psychological Association, 2019; Sege et al., 2018).

Listening, Talking, and Discussing

One of the most useful ways to achieve healthy child development is to promote using words instead of actions—and this can be done very early in children's lives. Increasing the children's capacity to put words to feelings and actions results in increased tension regulation (awareness of feelings and ability to tolerate them without having to act), self-awareness, and thoughtful decision-making. This process is accomplished by:

- Talking and using words instead of actions—talk rather than hit. Discuss with children what is safe or dangerous, what behaviors are acceptable or not, and why.
- Listening to children—find out why they did or did not do something.
- Explaining your reasons—this will enhance children's decision-making capacities.

The word *discipline* comes from the Latin word for "understanding," "teaching," or "learning." I prefer the words *understanding*, *teaching*, and *learning* because the word *discipline* in English tends toward *punishment*. Children's behaviors have meaning, and behaviors are directly connected to inner feelings. Thus, these processes of understanding, teaching, and learning are best seen as focusing on feelings and the behaviors that result from these feelings. Having realistic expectations of the level of self-control, patience, and judgment of a child at a given developmental stage greatly enhances a healthy sense of self and good interpersonal skills.

Labeling Feelings

Help children label their feelings with words as early as possible. Feelings such as interest, enjoyment, surprise, distress, anger, fear, shame, disgust, and dissmell can be labeled with words. This facilitates tension regulation and aids the transition to more mature ways of handling emotion. Encouraging the feeling of curiosity (interest) can be especially effective.

Positive Reinforcement

Rewards and praise will enhance the child's self-esteem when appropriate standards are met. Positive reinforcement is much more effective in obtaining short-term and long-term behavioral changes than punishments that evoke fear and shame. Positive affects enhance change more readily than negative affects.

Teaching by Example

Set a good example for the child. The child wants to be like the parents. Children identify with their parents, and they will put feelings and actions into words when they see their parents doing this. Who the parents are and how they behave will have a profound impact on the development of their children. A child will follow the parent's lead.

Parents and Caregivers Taking Care of Themselves

An exhausted, overburdened, or stressed parent or caregiver is less patient and less able to strategize effective, nonphysical approaches to discipline. Alcohol use also dramatically decreases frustration tolerance and increases impulsivity and the likelihood of violence. Interactions with others and various forms of support can be very helpful to stressed-out parents.

Potential Solutions and Prevention of Physical Punishment—Society

How can affects, cognition, and language be combined to offer alternatives to physical punishment in society?

Affects

Increasing the public's understanding of how affects function can help parents, caregivers, teachers, and others in dealing with anger, distress, fear, and shame in youngsters of all ages. In addition, knowledge of affects can lead to greater comprehension of behaviors resulting from such feelings: delinquency, depression, and violence. Many of the programs in schools that teach youngsters and parents about feelings—such as Social Emotional Learning (SEL)—are based on affects (Cohen, 2021; Holinger, 2021).

Cognition

Here, I refer to the variety of information and data on the causes and prevention of physical punishment and the alternatives. Making this information available to all segments of society is a public health imperative. Again, public health initiatives such as smoking and seatbelts have been effective not only with individual behaviors but also with societal attitudes as well.

Language

With language, the variety of information and data on physical punishment and the alternatives must be increasingly communicated and available. We, as individuals and all policymakers, need to become aware of the best way to express the damage inflicted by physical punishment and the way words are used in forming laws controlling physical punishment. In addition, language interacts closely with cognition in dealing with legal issues and enacting laws concerning physical punishment and abuse. This combination of language and cognition is explored here as social policy.

Social Policy

Legal restraints to prohibit physical punishment need to be further employed (e.g., Block, 2013). These legal efforts need to be accompanied by programs that enhance knowledge of early development and aid parent-child relationships. As noted previously, in 2023 Representative Bonamici and Senator Murphy reintroduced the Protecting our Students in Schools Act of 2023 to prohibit corporal punishment in any school that receives federal funding.

What are the legal issues involving physical punishment? There is always tension between the rights of individuals and the rights of others. With physical punishment, this tension involves the rights of parents to raise their own children as they wish, as well as the rights of the child and society. I would suggest, consistent with the data, that the rights of the child and society should hold sway. We do not allow one adult to commit assault and battery on another—why should we allow an adult to hit their child who is smaller and in a vulnerable developmental period? As the data show, the consequences of physical punishment are negative.

Some have pointed out that laws preventing physical punishment may burden the state and lead to even more negative outcomes (e.g., Huntington, 2020). However, in several countries that have prohibited physical punishment, the penalties involve parental help and education about development, with good results (e.g., Durrant & Smith, 2011; Österman et al., 2014, 2018). In addition, there is a concept in legal matters called "the voice of the law." In other words, having a law on the books in itself enhances awareness and increases thoughtfulness about the nature of the behavior in question, even if such a law is difficult to enforce. All this would suggest that laws prohibiting physical punishment should continue to be enacted internationally.

Summarizing

There does seem to be progress, albeit slow, in recognizing and dealing with the problem of physical punishment and its violence. Internationally, there appears to be increasing knowledge in this area and a groundswell to prohibit the hitting of children. Over 125 countries have now prohibited physical punishment in schools, and 64 countries have prohibited it in all settings. The follow-up data seem to suggest that these changes and laws have been beneficial. It would appear that group influence and the laws are creating some awareness and changes. Psychological advances may be involved, such as increased understanding of early development (with increased empathy for babies and children, recognizing differences from adults) and greater awareness of one's own childhood experiences and their impact on development.

Chapter 13

Toward Understanding Bias, Prejudice, and Violence

Chapter Outline:

- Cults: Religious and ideological
- Similar or different?
- Origins and dynamics of bias and prejudice: The interplay of affects, cognition, and language
- Bias, prejudice, and violence—In individuals
- Bias, prejudice, and violence—In groups and society
- How do people become prejudiced?
- Two cases: Derek Black and Jvonne Hubbard

Bias, prejudice, and violence and the resulting individual and group behaviors are complicated topics that have engaged not only philosophers, researchers, and politicians for years but also psychologists such as Sigmund Freud, Vamik Volkan, Elisabeth Young-Bruehl, and many others (see Strozier et al., 2010; Lifton, 2020). But rarely have those issues of "cultism and zealotry" (Lifton, 2020) been examined from the point of view of the impact that early development and affect, cognition, and language have on their germination and expression.

When looking at groups that embrace violence (such as the Islamic State [ISIS], Ku Klux Klan [KKK], Nazis, jihadists, Proud Boys, QAnon, and white supremacists) and at the individuals within those groups, it is important to ask how their members came to join the group and what they feel aligning themselves with those "causes" does for them. This can help us develop strategies that reduce or eliminate the damage caused by these groups and their members' behaviors. These strategies include making changes from the top down (that is, through social policy and in social groups) and the bottom up (through helping individuals who are drawn to those groups to change).

This is not intended as a comprehensive overview of those dynamics but as an introduction to how understanding early development and affect, cognition, and language can enhance the capacities of individuals, therapists, and society to change harmful beliefs and actions.

DOI: 10.4324/9780429203640-16

Bias, prejudice, and violence exist on a spectrum:

- *Bias* suggests an inclination or outlook.
- *Prejudice* is defined as an adverse opinion or learning formed without just grounds or before sufficient knowledge; an irrational attitude of hostility directed against an individual, group, or their supposed characteristics.
- *Violence* describes the exertion of physical force so as to injure or abuse.

This trio of emotional states can lead people to groups that soothe their distress and help vent their roiling anger. Often, those groups look like cults to outsiders, but to insiders, they look like long-sought answers to unhappiness.

Cults: Religious and Ideological

"We have to ask why cultism, both religious and ideological, is so persistent, why it appears and reappears in endless forms," writes Robert Jay Lifton (2020, p. 419). Lifton notes two important sources for cultism within the human psyche:

> The first has to do with the very prolonged period of human helplessness and dependency ... that tendency can also find expression in a need for an omnipotent guide with greater power even than that of one's parents.
>
> (p. 419)

The second is the ever-present issue of death for human beings.

> We have an uneasy awareness of death and spend our lives struggling with that awareness. The omnipotent guide, the sacred guru, offers a vision of overcoming death, of living in the eternal, of transcendent mystical experiences in which time and death disappear.
>
> (pp. 419–420)

Photo 13.1 Robert Jay Lifton
Source: Photograph by Wolfgang Richter

In other words, Lifton suggests two prominent motivations that attract people to cults. The first involves attachment (connection) and idealization. The second speaks to an apocalyptic or utopian view that can help fend off the fear of nonexistence, death, and the absence of stimulation. Both of these involve an effort of humans to shift from negative affects of distress and fear to positive affects of interest and enjoyment (and a decrease in tension). This is the view of the rock bottom, the individual basics. Although these basic needs are shared by all humans, only some find comfort in cults and outsider groups. So we have to look beyond that.

There are additional precipitants of cultism. For instance, many cults are triggered by unbearable and chaotic social circumstances and suffering—food and water shortages, poor health conditions, unemployment and financial instability, and social and political upheaval. Some cults form in reaction to threats to a group's convictions, including a perceived threat to comforting tenants of their religion—such as an afterlife and perpetual existence. These various developments can trigger intense negative affects, such as distress, fear, and anger. Cults can also be enhanced by positive affects—interest and enjoyment. Cults can help members achieve validation of self, a shared sense of purpose, and camaraderie.

Similar or Different?

In trying to understand groups that embrace prejudice, fear, and, often, violence, we need to ask whether groups such as QAnon and ISIS, Proud Boys and KKK are similar, different, or both. They appear similar with respect to their processes (that is, the affects, psychodynamics, and motivations) and different in terms of the specific targets and goals (for instance, white ascendency, repression of women, supremacy of a specific religion) and degree of violence. And any one group may have characteristics that embrace both similarities and differences.

Similarities

Many cults often bring together people who are experiencing varying degrees of negative affects such as distress, fear, and shame, sometimes with responses of rage and violence. Recently, there has been an increasing focus in the literature on the role of shame as "a crucial catalyst for ideologically motivated group violence" (Strozier & Mart, 2017, p. 23; Strozier et al., 2010).

For instance, many scholars suggest the humiliation of Germany's loss in World War I and the Treaty of Versailles contributed prominently to Hitler's rise and World War II. To this point, the historian Volker Ullrich (2020) writes that

> As the site for the signing of the . . . [capitulation of France to Germany, June 21, 1940] . . . Hitler had chosen the very clearing in the forest of Compiègne where the German delegation . . . had formally ended hostilities in the First World War on 11 November 1918. To that end, the salon carriage in which the signing ceremony had taken place back then was located and brought to the precise spot

in which it had stood in 1918. Every detail of the signing event was staged. The message was unmistakable: the ceremony of 21 June 1940 was an act of revenge for the lost war of 1914–18 and the "humiliation" of the treaty of Versailles.

(p. 108)

Hitler's face was afire with scorn, anger, hate, revenge, and triumph, according to William Shirer, CBS correspondent. Hitler described the choice of location as an "act of restorative justice . . . to extinguish a memory . . . that was considered by the German people as the deepest humiliation of all time" (p. 109). That evening, Hitler discussed the events with Goebbels: "Our humiliation has now been erased" (p. 109). This process involves what Tomkins describes as a damage-reparation script, which deals especially with the affect of shame, resulting in rage and violence.

The various cult-like groups also tend to elevate their members above outsiders, inflate members' sense of self-worth, mobilize fear of the "Other," and then attempt to annihilate the "Other" in one fashion or another. Hitler's antisemitism provides an example. Albert Speers remembered one characteristic scene. On a walk together, Hitler suddenly began yelling:

We will get our hands on them! Then we will settle accounts! Then they will find out who I really am! This time none of them will escape! I have always been too kind-hearted! Not any more! Now it is time to settle accounts!

(Ullrich, 2020, p. 612)

The positive affects of interest and enjoyment are also apparent, and the benefits of joining a group seem similar from group to group. These groups give the members a sense of belonging, of being understood and validated. The affects of interest and enjoyment enhance members' sense of self-cohesion and give them a sense of purpose, often by bestowing each member with a sense of superiority over others outside the group. In addition, the "togetherness" of fighting a common enemy, an outlet for anger and rage, and a utopian vision—sometimes of life after death—are all enticing to people who are struggling to find their place in the world, self-acceptance, hope, and love. Utopian or apocalyptic visions are common in many groups, including in mainstream religions (Strozier et al., 2010).

Differences

What are the differences between groups? There appear to be three major issues—the targets (victims) of the perpetrators, the degree of violence involved, and the size of the groups.

First, the targets may be picked for various "reasons"—ethnic, racial, political, ideological, gender, religion, and so on. One group may target immigrants, whereas others target Muslims, infidels, and people of color. Targets may have a particular form of "otherness" that becomes a focus of fear and anger. For one, group facial features may elicit anger, and for other groups, skin color, ethnicity, customs, body shapes and sizes (e.g., big/small, fat/thin, tall/short), religion, gender, wealth, language, education, or class and status may be associated with some degree of antagonism, even violence. What psychological, social, physical, and historical variables account for an individual or group focusing on one or another of these qualities is an important question in understanding the underlying motives and dynamics.

Second, the degree of aggression against the target may be quite different between groups. Some may, at times, use words, lawyers, and courts to pursue their attack on others, as a hate-fueled Washington politician may do. Other groups may use varying degrees of violence, torture, or all-out war to accomplish their goals.

Third, the groups tend to differ significantly in size. Some involve the populations of entire countries, whereas others are quite limited—such as Jim Jones and his evangelistic Peoples Temple in Jonestown, Guyana, and David Koresh and the Branch Davidians in Waco, Texas.

Origins and Dynamics of Bias and Prejudice: The Interplay of Affects, Cognition, and Language

Human beings and other animals developed the abilities to perceive and react to differences because these processes are essential to evolution, adaptation, and survival. Living things, in one way or another, perform many pattern-matching activities that call out differences (Basch, 1988). Is this thing approaching me dangerous? Is it familiar or different? Will it hurt me? Is it too big? Will it try to eat me? Or can I eat it? Can we be friends? Or just leave each other alone?

The perception of differences allows humans to predict, sort out cause and effect, pursue alternatives, and so on. The process involves creating order out of all the myriad of stimuli with which we are confronted. Recent research suggests this categorization starts early. Already at four months, babies can distinguish between animate and inanimate objects (Spriet et al., 2022). Affects, cognition, and language are all involved in this pattern-matching and sorting-out process. Language becomes a vehicle for expression of the emotions and thoughts that affects and cognition produce.

Creating order out of disorder is one of the primary functions of the brain, and assessing the nature of differences in stimuli is a large part of that. But that impulse can backfire—and many people end up having a great deal of trouble with differences. In a peaceful, secure world, differences can be a source of curiosity, exploration, and enjoyment. In an insecure, frightening world, they may be a source of fear, envy, and rage, potential dangers to be avoided or battled.

In dealing with differences, two processes are especially important: *innate capacities* (including affects) and *learning* (including cognition). There is overlap, and it is not always easy to determine what is innate and what is learned.

The *innate capacities* relevant to this discussion consist of two components. The first concerns the inborn ability to assess the nature of incoming stimuli—i.e., are they familiar or different, do the patterns match or not, and what affects are triggered? The second is *temperament*, defined as biologically based individual differences in emotional and motor reactivity and self-regulation that demonstrate consistency across situations over time; temperament can be modulated by environmental factors.

The *learning* process also consists of two components. The first component includes information that comes into a person from the outside world, such as nonverbal indications from the environment (*social referencing*), verbal learning (being told something verbally), and formal education. The second entails what is learned by individuals through their own experiences that are the result of outward action, interaction, and reaction. Thus, innate factors as well as learned processes contribute to how humans respond to differences/otherness and what affects (e.g., interest or fear) are elicited. *In other words, bias and prejudice seem to result from the impact of early (and later) learning and experiences on the innate capacities of each individual's affect system.*

In Chapter 3 (Figure 3.3), I discussed what happens when any stimulus—a pinprick, bright light, loud noise—impinges upon an infant or an adult (Tomkins, 1991). The affects of surprise, fear, and interest are evoked depending on the rate of stimulus increase a person experiences and neural firing. For example, the surprise response may be followed by either fear or interest. Which way it goes depends on how a person's cognitive processes sort out the nature of the stimulus—is it familiar or not, how different is it from other stimuli, is it dangerous or beneficial?

As Tomkins puts it: "It is not uncommon for startle to be followed by terror, but it may be followed by excitement depending on the outcome of poststartle scanning" (1991, p. 495). Tomkins's term "poststartle scanning" refers to the capacity of animals, including humans, to assess present stimuli and circumstances, compare them to the past, and anticipate and predict: "Presumably, there must be a sufficient cognitive complexity to enable the animal to create a matrix of anticipations independent of the actual presence of the original terrifying scene" (1991, p. 497).

Here is where pattern-matching, differences, and learned experience quickly become important (Basch, 1988). Affects are innate responses to stimuli, but what stimuli trigger what affects appears to be significantly influenced by experience and learning—that is, cognition (see Kelly et al., 2005). For some people, certain stimuli can elicit fear and lead to bias and prejudice and to anger, rage, and violence. But, those same stimuli, if shaped by positive cognitive processes, can instead lead to a response of interest and enjoyment rather than fear in other people (see Chapter 3).

Bias, Prejudice, and Violence—In Individuals

Let's look more closely at bias, prejudice, and violence through the lenses of affects, cognition, and language, exploring both individual and group dynamics (while appreciating the close interactions of individuals and groups as discussed in the "Introduction to Part 2").

Affects

In individuals, fear and other negative affects seem central to understanding bias and prejudice. Fear is very toxic and is designed for emergency motivation. Tomkins differentiates fear from distress, the latter being evoked for a longer period of time and felt as burdensome (1992). Distress and fear and all the other negative affects—anger, shame, disgust, dissmell, alone or in combination—have the capacity to trigger increasing rage and violence toward any number of targets, depending on the individuals or the group.

The psychodynamics involved have been described in a variety of ways, often depending on the psychological school of thought and the specific affect involved. For example, we often hear the following terms associated with perpetrators of violence due to bias and prejudice: fragile sense of self-esteem, feelings of inferiority, and compensatory grandiosity; lack of self-cohesion (impaired internal order leading to fear and distress). They are described as wounded, shamed, and humiliated; as expressing various current or past traumas, experiencing individual or societal deprivation, and being overwhelmed by the need for revenge (and a rageful effort to gain empathy: "See, this is how it feels!").

The issue of power is at stake here, along with anger and rage. A fragile sense of self-esteem is often dealt with by having power over someone or something else. I've seen this frequently in children and adolescents as well as adults. For instance, bullies pick on weaker children and firm up their own self-esteem in the process. There may be an identification with a powerful, sometimes raging person—with the strength and capacities of that person. The need to hurt or control another person may be primary to the stabilizing of the self-esteem of the aggressor and have little to do with aspects of the victim—or it may have a great deal to do with who and what the victim is.

This identification with the strong, aggressive person may occur even if a person disagrees with that strong person . . . it is the apparent strength, the power that is being identified with, not necessarily the goals or views of that person. This is discussed by Kernberg and others in regard to individuals and mass movements: "Their identification with the leader of the mass movement, which provides them with a sense of shared identity, an identification with the leader who is not only powerful and idealized, but also feared" (2020, p. 3).

I recently heard another example of the fear and anger underlying bias and prejudice. A man was asked in the midst of the pandemic why he wouldn't take the vaccine: "You are not going to shove that down my throat," he roared. Who is the "you"? What caused these feelings and responses, I have no idea—an early parental transference, a projection of some sort, previous experience, or something he had read or heard (e.g., misinformation)? But the fear and rage were palpable. Instead of seeing care, the desire to help protect him from peril, he saw the suggestion of a vaccine as an invasion of his hyper-defended personal space and sense of self. It appeared he felt any social or individual action entering his territory posed a threat. (One can only imagine how scary his childhood may have been.)

Cognition

When examining cognition in relationship to bias and prejudice, it's important to examine the interactions between affects and cognition and what is innate (affects) and what is learned (cognition), especially in the context of bias and prejudice.

Affects refer to innate responses to stimuli. Cognition refers to learning, processing, assessing the internal and external world, thinking, and self-awareness.

When a person is observing and reacting to differences and "otherness," both affects and cognition are involved. How children—and adults—respond affectively will be influenced by their innate reactivity and perception and also by what they have been told and experienced. Will they respond with positive or negative affects—curiosity and interest, or fear and anger?

Affects and cognition have both assets and liabilities (see Chapter 1). Each can impact the other profoundly. Affects can influence cognition: For example, consider, on the one hand, how anger and fear can—and often do—negatively impact cognition. In a rage, it is difficult to think clearly. And when overwhelmed with fear, careful thought gives way to fight or flight impulses. And conversely, interest (curiosity) can positively influence cognitive problem-solving and behavior in various circumstances. Using well-developed cognitive processes can lead to a deeper understanding of affects and enlarge an individual's behavioral responses to them.

Cognition can reshape affects and language in order to minimize bias and prejudice and violence. Two of our most influential contributors to the understanding of humanity promote the importance of cognition: Charles Darwin noted that "Great is the power of steady misrepresentation; but the history of science shows that fortunately this power does not long endure" (1859). And Sigmund Freud wrote: "The voice of the intellect is a soft one, but it does not rest till it has gained a hearing. Finally, after a countless succession of rebuff, it succeeds . . . in the long run, nothing can withstand reason and experience" (1927, pp. 53, 54).

Language

There are two aspects of language that I wish to mention in the context of bias, prejudice, and violence. The first involves written and spoken language as a weapon—sometimes a deadly weapon. Certain words, such as racial and ethnic slurs, can be wounding, hurtful, and potentially destructive. Language can undermine a child's development and sense of self when it elicits distress, fear, shame, self-disgust, and rage in the context of bias and prejudice. In children and adults, language can be used to elicit both negative and positive affects in the name of bias and prejudice to motivate groups toward violence and great destructiveness.

Second, when language is joined with positive affect expression and cognition that has the power to evaluate and see otherness as nonthreatening, it can counteract bias and prejudice and enhance empathy and healing—that is, the pen can be mightier than the sword.

Fictionalized as well as research-driven and personal accounts have had a profound impact on the public's understanding of bias and prejudice—for example, Harriet Beecher Stowe's *Uncle Tom's Cabin*, Frederick Douglass's three autobiographies (including *Narrative of the Life of Frederick Douglass, an American Slave*), Elie Wiesel's *Night*, John Howard Griffin's *Black Like Me*, Robert Jay Lifton's *The Nazi Doctors*, and finally the books by two ex-white supremacists, Derek Black's *Rising Out of Hatred* and Jvonne Hubbard's *White Sheets to Brown Babies*. As noted shortly, the words spoken and written by Lincoln, Martin Luther King, Jr., and others have had important positive effects on society. In addition, in our era of recordings, video, and social media, the pictures and words involved in countering bias and prejudice can be profoundly impactful. Consider George Floyd and "I can't breathe," "Black Lives Matter," and #MeToo.

Bias, Prejudice, and Violence—In Groups and Society

In this section, I turn to bias, prejudice, and violence at the group and societal level.

Affects

David Terman integrated affects (especially fear, shame, and anger) with the fundamentalist mindset and violence (2010a). Terman suggests that most of these fundamentalist groups have a very specific set of dynamics, which he calls the *paranoid gestalt*. "It is a general perceptual, affective-cognitive organization in individuals and an analogous, shared cognitive structure in groups. The pattern is quite stereotypic, and this invariant regularity is most evident in groups" (2010a, p. 47). Although there are varying degrees of paranoia among the individuals, the group has a conviction that there is a malevolent conspiracy against it. Utopian visions are also common. "Along with the more recent work on paranoia," Terman noted, "I have placed much less emphasis on projection and have given much greater attention to the issues of shame and humiliation" (p. 51). For example, recall the historian Volker Ullrich highlighting the importance of Hitler's emphasizing Germany's shame and humiliation post-Versailles as he built up the Nazi party in the 1930s (2016). In addition, there is often the notion that this "evil other" must be exterminated (what Tomkins terms a *decontamination script* powered by disgust [1992]), with a utopia of some sort being the result (2010b; Terman, personal communication, 2021). These ideas may be taught from birth, or they may arise due to narcissistic injuries, humiliation, poor socioeconomic conditions, war, need for revenge, fear, hate, and so on.

Another topic that should be noted within the context of affects involves the violence associated with bias and prejudice. The contagion of affect was discussed previously, as various excessive negative affects can lead to anger, rage, and violent behaviors. Sometimes, the violence occurs within a relatively brief period of time—as members of one group are killed, provoking trauma and pain, the other group retaliates, and the cycle continues for a few months to years. This type of contagion can be within a generation as *intragenerational violence*. It is seen frequently in urban gang conflicts.

Another variation takes place over longer periods of time and over several generations. The rage and need for revenge continue for decades or even centuries and is transferred from one generation to the next. Termed *intergenerational violence*, it often involves the intermingling of politics and religion.

Intergenerational violence also occurs in families beset by physical punishment. Those who are subjected to physical punishment are much more likely to use it against others, and it gets passed on from generation to generation (Holden, 2020).

The focus thus far has been on the function of negative affects in bias, prejudice, and violence. However, as previously mentioned, positive affects are also involved, and they deserve further mention. Groups such as the KKK, ISIS, and the Nazis appear to be motivated by a complex mixture of positive and negative affects. The groups give vent to the negative affects and offer substitutions for missing positive ones. Cults and anti-social groups provide validation, attention, and positive affects of interest and enjoyment to people who are often missing them. For instance, consider the longing for closeness, belonging, attachment, and organization; the decrease in tension (enjoyment) when you are appreciated, understood, and validated; and the sense of order when there is a shared purpose and goals.

These positive aspects of groups will become important when discussing the changes some people make as they leave these groups. The positive affects associated with groups are often instrumental in enticing people to join a violent cult—and also to leave it for a different group. This is discussed in what follows in the cases of Derek Black (Saslow, 2018) and Jvonne Hubbard (2018).

Leaders can be very influential with respect to bias, prejudice, and violence. I briefly discuss leaders here due to their capacity to enhance both positive and negative affects on individuals and groups. The oft-debated question, "Do the times make the leader, or does the leader make the times?" seems dependent on specific situations and a host of variables. Ullrich gives an example of this involving Adolf Hitler:

> Without Hitler, the rise of National Socialism would have been unthinkable . . . Nonetheless, the special conditions of the immediate post-war years were also crucial: without the explosive mixture of economic misery, social instability and collective trauma, the popular agitator Hitler would never have been able to work his way out of anonymity to become a famous politician.
>
> (2016, p. 92)

However, regardless of the leader or circumstances question, there is no doubt about the power of some leaders to use positive and negative affects to motivate their followers and enhance their causes. Hitler could elicit excitement and joy, and he was a master at eliciting fear, disgust, and rage in his audiences.

Consider also some leaders who have used various means to elicit interest and enjoyment and inspire a sense of togetherness that undermined bias and prejudice.

Abraham Lincoln

- Gettysburg Address (November 19, 1863): "We here highly resolve that these dead shall not have died in vain—that this nation, under God, shall have a new birth of freedom—and that the government of the people, by the people, and for the people shall not perish from the earth."[1]
- Second Inaugural Address (March 4, 1865): "With malice toward none; with charity for all; . . . let us strive on to finish the work we are in; . . . to do all which may achieve and cherish a just and lasting peace among ourselves, and with all nations."[2]

Franklin D. Roosevelt

- In his First Inaugural Address (March 4, 1933), Roosevelt used a nice twist to decrease fear and enhance interest during the Depression with his phrase: "the only thing we have to fear is . . . fear itself—nameless, unreasoning, unjustified terror." With these words, Roosevelt introduced curiosity and cognition into the issue of fear.[3]

Martin Luther King, Jr.

- "I Have a Dream" Speech (August 28, 1963): "I have a dream that one day on the red hills of Georgia, the sons of former slaves and the sons of former slave owners will be able to sit down together at the table of brotherhood . . . I have a dream that my four little children will one day live in a nation where they will not be judged by the color of their skin but by the content of their character. I have a dream today."[4]

Cognition

And yet, here we are, some 80 years from the German's Nazi propaganda, dealing with anti-vax theories in the midst of the COVID-19 pandemic, the QAnon conspiracy, climate-change opponents, and significant bias, prejudice, and racism. Politicians and those creating public policy, therapists, and interested individuals might do well to focus on and learn as much as possible about affects and cognition, their development, their functions, and how they interact—their usefulness as a checks-and-balance feedback system, one which allows for an enhancement of individual and group curiosity and diminishment of fear.

Education appears essential to efforts to prevent the harm caused by bias, prejudice, and violence—but such education appears underemphasized and often misdirected. First, there needs to be a greater understanding of the processes underlying bias and prejudice, as has been described throughout this chapter.

Second, the evolutionary, migratory, biological, and environmental forces that create differences in color, ethnicity, facial features, and so on need far more understanding and visibility than they are getting. It is not enough to know that humans have different characteristics. We must also learn what underlies these differences and mixtures, that is, what causes humans to have different skin colors, body types, facial features, or various attributes and liabilities. Adam Rutherford discusses these issues extensively in his book *How to Argue with a Racist: What Our Genes Do (and Don't) Say About Human Difference* (2020).

Third, promoting critical thinking, creativity, scientific methodology, exposure to various topics and data, and so on, are important at all levels. And we might benefit from enhancing interest and enjoyment—curiosity and empathy—at every turn, from early development onward.

Language

The words that record and make public the laws of the land can be transformative—this was discussed earlier in the section on physical punishment. The legal processes, with words articulating various aspects of behaviors and consequences, are crucial. In addition, the "voice of the law," having laws on the books and in the public eye, can itself be useful in alerting individuals and society to the serious problems associated with bias, prejudice, and violence.

However, in prejudiced and tyrannical governments, laws can be detrimental and contribute to severe and destructive discrimination of individuals and society—consider the Jim Crow laws in the United States, the Taliban and Islamic laws restricting women's lives in Afghanistan, and the antisemitic laws of Germany in the 1930s–1945.

How Do People Become Prejudiced?

So, I end up with this one central question: How do people become prejudiced?

I discussed how early the seeds of bias, prejudice, and violence can be sown and how two aspects of affect (inborn capacity of affects to assess differences in stimuli, and one's temperament) and two aspects of cognition (what one is taught and what one experiences) may contribute to individual fear and rage and social prejudice. And as Adam Rutherford noted, "Structural racism is everyday—and rooted in the everyday. It is rooted in indifference to the lived experience of the recipients of racism" (2020, p. 6).

In individuals, affect and cognition may interact to produce increased vulnerability to prejudice—consider the impact of parents, caregivers, and communities that are prejudiced or anxious and create a "stranger-danger" atmosphere in raising their children: Things (and people) that are different are to be feared and/or despised. Being mistreated, marginalized, or bullied inside or outside the home are risk factors for prejudice and violence. Narcissistic problems (e.g., fragile self-esteem, shame), depression, distress, fear, setbacks in life, loss of purpose, and other dynamics may lead to a need to project and blame in order to protect or enhance oneself, with resultant bias and prejudice.

In general, underlying bias and prejudice involve excessive negative affects and diminished positive affects, whether early in life or later. Much is known about the psychopathology and treatment of these individuals, groups, and leaders, but much is still to be learned (for example, Kohut, 1971; Kernberg, 1975, 1984; Basch, 1988; Meloy, 2001; Kimmel, 2013, 2018).

In groups and societies, social conditions can create fertile soil for nourishing bias, prejudice, and violence. It turns out that as adaptive and flexible as humans are, they are also fragile. When society does not offer security, esteem, and affirmation, then various groups within it splinter, and members feel the need to protect themselves from outside dangers. The remedy to this can only come from the top down—with economic, social, and political structures that let people calm down, reduce their sense of threat, and allow them to begin to feel generous to others as society is generous to them.

Social deprivations are apparent frequently in situations marked by bias, prejudice, and violence. And from social deprivations emerge distress, fear, rage, shame, and disgust, along with a desire for control, power, and greed. Leaders are influential in these circumstances—for instance, consider the pathology of Hitler (Ullrich, 2016) and Stalin. And yet there are examples of positive change subsequent to horrible conditions: for example, the work of Lucius D. Clay and the Marshall Plan in Germany, and Douglas MacArthur in Japan after World War II.

In creating change, politicians and personnel attempting to decrease the prejudice and violence of these groups may find it useful to understand the dynamics of these groups' specific fears, the shame, rage, and depravations that drive their behaviors and fantasies. In addition, a focus on understanding malevolent leaders—their goals, attributes, and pathology—may be beneficial. Ongoing efforts to make contact may be valuable in creating the possibility of alliance, containment, and change. Advances are possible through education of the groups and their members about solutions to their social circumstances and various aspects of possible assistance.

Two Cases: Derek Black and Jvonne Hubbard

Let's close with two cases that deserve mention in this discussion: Derek Black (Saslow, 2018, *Rising Out of Hatred: The Awakening of a Former White Nationalist*) and Jvonne Hubbard (*White Sheets to Brown Babies*, 2018). Both were raised by white supremacists, and both ultimately repudiated this stance. Black's father founded the largest racist community on the internet, and his godfather was David Duke, a KKK Grand Wizard. Derek himself became an extremely popular figure and leading light of the white nationalist movement.

Jvonne Hubbard was indoctrinated by her father, the Grand Dragon of a faction of the KKK, to hate minorities. When she was seven, she rode in the car with her father and was told to

> lay down on the back floorboard . . . dad was riddling someone's car with multiple bullets . . . On the second occasion . . . I rose just in time to see my dad

Photo 13.2 Jvonne Hubbard and her father, Joel Hubbard
Source: Jvonne Hubbard

was holding a glass soda bottle with a rag sticking out of the top that he lit on fire and threw like a bomb through someone's front window. I actually saw their curtains go up in flames . . . it had been the home of a young white woman who had a black baby. If I had been afraid of my dad before, let me tell you I was terrified now.

(2018, p. 9)

Both began to question their beliefs in late adolescence and early adulthood. For Derek Black, this occurred when he went to college and was befriended by a group of fellow college students, including some who were Jewish. He also fell in love with a female classmate who began to get him to question his cognitive rationales for his prejudices. Jvonne was frequently in trouble with the law during her adolescence. Ultimately, she was incarcerated and taken under the wing of older African-American women, and in that context, she began to heal and become less enraged, giving up her white supremacist views. Later, she adopted a biracial baby (hence the title of her book).

My colleague Kalia Doner and I interviewed Jvonne. We found her to be wonderfully open and thoughtful about her life and transition. She noted that the hatred instilled in her during her early years was particularly burdensome. In both these cases, positive affects and emotions—understanding and empathy, kindness, love, validation—nurtured by the people they met at a university and in jail were essential to their transformations.

Notes

1 Abraham Lincoln Online, www.abrahamlincolnonline.org/lincoln/speeches/gettysburg.htm
2 National Park Service, www.nps.gov/linc/learn/historyculture/lincoln-second-inaugural.htm
3 *American Experience,* PBS, www.pbs.org/wgbh/americanexperience/features/fdr-first-inaugural/
4 Changing Minds.org, http://changingminds.org/analysis/i_have_a_dream.htm

Chapter 14

Wrapping Up and a Glance at the Future

In looking back at this book, I can identify three central messages. First, I highlight the increasing awareness of the remarkable capacities of infants and children and their overall social connectedness. By appreciating these attributes, I believe we have a better chance of understanding how we can enhance human development as parents, clinicians, and participants in society.

The second major message involves the three essential information systems—affects, cognition, language—and their interactions. Advances in our understanding of these information systems can provide a foundation for further enhancement of individual development, clinical work, and social relations.

Third, I suggest that a deeper understanding of these information systems can have an impact on some of our most troubling social problems. To this end, I discuss the serious problems caused by both physical punishment as well as bias, prejudice, and violence, and how a comprehensive understanding of the roles of affects, cognition, and language can lead to potential solutions.

A Glance at the Future

In wrapping up, I am intrigued by the long view. Scientists now tell us that the universe is approximately 13.77 billion years old, and the Earth is about 4.54 billion years old. Paleontologists note that over 99 percent of all species that ever lived on the Earth are now extinct. Evolution involves changes in the inherited traits of a population through successive generations, and it contains the potential capacity to adapt to local circumstances. Evolutionary processes in species may take eons.

Charles Darwin had a lovely way of expressing these processes in a paragraph toward the end of *Origin of Species*:

> It is interesting to contemplate an entangled bank, clothed with many plants of many kinds, with birds singing on the bushes, with various insects flitting about, and with worms crawling through the damp earth, and to reflect that these elaborately constructed forms, so different from each other, and dependent on each other in so complex a manner, have all been produced by laws acting around us.
>
> (1859, p. 489)

DOI: 10.4324/9780429203640-17

We are a young species—approximately 300,000 years old. Human beings today confront growing populations, incessant wars, climate changes, the possibility of nuclear war, and radioactivity. Wouldn't it be interesting to see what happens to humans over the next several thousands and millions of years? How might human beings adapt and evolve in the face of variables and changes in their environment? Will the neurobiological aspects of affects, cognition, and language be altered and evolve over time? For example, Tomkins raises an interesting issue: "It is an open question whether the capacity for gross terror, incompatible as it is with the concurrent exercise of complex cognitive functions is still as useful for an animal such as man" (1991, p. 498). Are our cognitive capacities and understanding of affects up to the task?

Perhaps, in the meantime, we could do worse than recognize the assets and liabilities of affects, cognition, and language in development, clinical work, relationships, and societies—becoming increasingly self-aware, focusing on interest and curiosity, and using them to fuel our capacities for empathy. We might also do well to recall a small segment of Abraham Lincoln's Annual Message to Congress on December 1, 1862, delivered a month before he signed the Emancipation Proclamation and when he was in the midst of trying to preserve the Union and end slavery:

> We can succeed only by concert. It is not "Can any of us imagine better" but "Can we all do better?" Object whatsoever is possible, still the question recurs, "Can we do better?"[1]

Note

1 A. Lincoln, Second Annual Message, The American Presidency Project, December 1, 1862, www.presidency.ucsb.edu/documents/second-annual-message-9

References

Abbasi, J. (2019). American Academy of Pediatrics says no more spanking or harsh verbal discipline. *Journal of the American Medical Association, 321*(5), 437–439.

Adler, G., & Buie, D. (1979). Aloneness and borderline psychopathology: The possible relevance of child development issues. *International Journal Psychoanalysis, 60*, 83–96.

Aichhorn, A. (1925). *Wayward youth*. Internationale, Psychoanalytischer Verlog.

Ainsworth, M., Blehar, M. C., Waters, E., & Wall, S. N. (1978). *Patterns of attachment: Observations in the strange situation and at home*. Lawrence Erlbaum Associates.

Akhtar, S. (2017). Open-mouthed and wide-eyed: Psychoanalytic reflections on curiosity. *Journal of the American Psychoanalytic Association, 65*(5), 264–304.

American Psychological Association. (2019, February). *Resolution on physical discipline by parents*. American Psychological Association.

APsA Position Statement on Physical Punishment. (2021). https://apsa.org/wp-content/uploads/2022/02/CorporalPunishment.pdf

Arato, A., & Gebhardt, E. (Eds.). (1982). *The essential Frankfurt School reader*. Continuum.

Arendt, H. (1966). *The origins of totalitarianism*. Harcourt, Brace, & World, Inc.

Aristotle. (2002). *Nicomachean ethics* (J. Sachs, ed.). Focus Publishers, R. Pullins.

Bacal, H. A., & Newman, K. M. (1990). *Theories of object relations: Bridges to self psychology*. Columbia University Press.

Basch, M. F. (1976). The concept of affect: A re-examination. *Journal of the American Psychoanalytic Association, 24*(4), 759–777. https://doi.org/10.1177/000306517602400401

Basch, M. F. (1983a). Empathic understanding: A review of the concept and some theoretical considerations. *Journal of the American Psychoanalytic Association, 31*(1), 101–126. https://doi.org/10.1177/000306518303100104

Basch, M. F. (1983b). The perception of reality and the disavowal of meaning. *The Annual of Psychoanalysis, 11*, 125–153.

Basch, M. F. (1988). *Understanding psychotherapy: The science behind the art*. Basic Books.

Basch, M. F. (1991). The significance of a theory of affect for psychoanalytic technique. *Journal of the American Psychoanalytic Association, 39*(Suppl.), 291–304.

Beiser, H. R. (1984). On curiosity: A developmental approach. *Journal of the American Academy of Child Psychiatry, 23*(5), 517–526. https://doi.org/10.1016/S0002-7138(09)60341-1

Beiser, H. R. (1989). Fatherhood and the preference for a younger child. *Annual of Psychoanalysis, 17*, 203–212.

Beiser, H. R. (1995). A follow-up of child analysis: The analyst as a real person. *The Psychoanalytic Study of the Child, 50*(1), 106–121. https://doi.org/10.1080/00797308.1995.11822398

Bion, W. R. (1959). *Experiences in groups and other papers*. Basic Books, Inc.

References

Bitensky, S. H. (2006). *Corporal punishment of children: A human rights violation.* Transnational Publishers, Inc.

Block, N. (2013). *Breaking the paddle: Ending school corporal punishment.* Center for Effective Discipline.

Blumenthal, S. (2016). *A self-made man: The political life of Abraham Lincoln, vol. 1, 1809–1849.* Simon & Schuster.

Bowlby, J. (1969). *Attachment: Vol. I. Attachment and loss.* Basic Books.

Brinich, P., & Gilmore, K. (2002). Panel: Child psychoanalysis: Cathecting and verbalising affects in a new relationship. Aspects of the analytic method in work with children. *International Journal of Psychoanalysis, 83*(Pt. 2), 473–477. https://doi.org/10.1516/y8p0-bbqn-3c9l-4xau

Browne, J. (2002). *Charles Darwin: The power of place.* Princeton University Press.

Cavell, M. (2003). The intelligence of the emotions: A view from philosophy. *Journal of the American Psychoanalytic Association, 51*(3), 977–994. http://apa.sagepub.com/content/51/3/977

Cohen, J. (2021). School safety and violence. Research and clinical understandings, trends, and improvement strategies. *International Journal of Applied Psychoanalytic Studies, 18*(3), 252–263. https://doi.org/10.1002/aps.1718

Committee on the Rights of the Child, General Comment No. 8. (2006). *The right of the child to protection from corporal punishment and other cruel or degrading forms of punishment.* Convention on the Rights of the Child, CRC/C/GC/8*, 2 March 2007. www.refworld.org/docid/460bc7772.html

Cooper, S. H. (2023). *Playing and becoming in psychoanalysis.* Routledge.

Cranston, M. (1982). *Jean-Jacques. The early life and work of Jean-Jacques Rousseau 1712–1754.* University of Chicago Press.

Cuartas, J., Weissman, D. G., Sheridan, M. A., Lengua, L., & McLaughlin, K. A. (2021). Corporal punishment and elevated neural response to threat in children. *Child Development, 92*(3), 821–832. https://doi.org/10.1111/cdev.13565

Damasio, A. R. (2003). *Looking for Spinoza: Joy, sorrow, and the feeling brain.* Harcourt.

Darwin, C. (1859). *On the origin of species by means of natural selection, or the preservation of favoured races in the struggle for life.* John Murray.

Darwin, C. (1871). *The descent of man, and selection in relation to sex* (1st ed.). John Murray; *The descent of man and selection in relation to sex* (2nd ed.). John Murray, 1874. Quotes from 2nd edition, Prometheus Books, 1998.

Darwin, C. (1872a). *The expression of the emotions in man and animals* (K. Lorenz, ed., 2nd ed.). University of Chicago Press, 1965.

Darwin, C. (1872b). *The expression of the emotions in man and animals* (P. Ekman, ed., 3rd ed.). Oxford University Press, 1998.

Darwin, C. (1877). A biographical sketch of an infant. *Mind: Quarterly Review of Psychology and Philosophy, 2,* 285–294.

Darwin, C. (1881). *The life and letters of Charles Darwin* (F. Darwin, ed.). https://charles-darwin.classic-literature.co.uk/the-life-and-letters-of-charles-darwin-volume-i/ebook-page-42.asp

Demos, E. V. (1989). A prospective constructionist view of development. *Annual Psychoanalysis, 17,* 287–308.

Demos, E. V. (1994, May). *Links between mother-infant transactions and the infant's psychic organization* [Paper presented to the Chicago Psychoanalytic Society].

Demos, E. V. (1995). *Exploring affect: The selected writings of Silvan S. Tomkins.* Cambridge University Press.

Demos, E. V. (2019). *The affect theory of Silvan Tomkins for psychoanalysis and psychotherapy: Recasting the essentials.* Routledge.

de Waal, F. (2019). *Mama's last hug: Animal emotions and what they tell us about ourselves*. W. W. Norton & Company.
Durrant, J. E. (2016). *Positive discipline in everyday parenting* (4th ed.). Save the Children.
Durrant, J. E., & Ensom, R. (2012). Physical punishment of children: Lessons from 20 years of research. *Canadian Medical Association Journal, 184*(12), 1373–1377.
Durrant, J. E., & Ensom, R. (2017). Twenty-five years of physical punishment research: What have we learned? *Journal of the Korean Academy of Child and Adolescent Psychiatry, 28*(1), 20–24. https://doi.org/10.5765/jkacap.2017.28.1.20
Durrant, J. E., & Smith, A. B. (Eds.). (2011). *Global pathways to abolishing physical punishment: Realizing children's rights*. Routledge.
Einstein, A. (1952). Letter to Carl Seelig, March 11, 1952.
Ekman, P. (Ed.). (1973). *Darwin and facial expression: A century of research in review*. Academic Press.
Ekman, P. (Ed.). (1998). *The expression of the emotions in man and animals* (C. Darwin, ed., 3rd ed.). Oxford University Press (Original work published 1872).
Ekman, P. (2003). *Emotions revealed: Recognizing faces and feelings to improve communication and emotional life*. Henry Holt and Company.
Fajardo, B. (1987). Neonatal trauma and early development. *Annual of Psychoanalysis, 15*, 233–244.
Ferro, A., & Meregnani, A. (1994). Rivista Di Psicoanalisi XXXVII, 1991; XXXVIII, 1992: Emotions, affects, personification. Eugenio Gaburri. Pp. 324–351. *Psychoanalytic Quarterly, 63*, 604–605.
Field, K., Cohler, B. J., & Wool, G. (Eds.). (1989). *Learning and education: Psychoanalytic perspectives*. International Universities Press.
Fonagy, P., Gergely, G., & Jurist, E. L. (2002). *Affect regulation, mentalization, and the development of the self*. Other Press.
Fonagy, P., & Target, M. (1996a). Playing with reality: I. Theory of mind and the normal development of psychic reality. *International Journal of Psychoanalysis, 77*(Pt. 2), 217–233.
Fonagy, P., & Target, M. (1996b). Predictors of outcome in child psychoanalysis: A retrospective study of 763 cases at the Anna Freud Centre. *Journal of the American Psychoanalytic Association, 44*(1), 27–77. https://doi.org/10.1177/000306519604400104
Fonagy, P., & Target, M. (1999). An interpersonal view of the infant. In A. Hurry (Ed.), *Psychoanalysis and developmental therapy* (pp. 3–31). International Universities Press.
Fortson, B. L., Klevens, J., Merrick, M. T., Gilbert, L. K., & Alexander, S. P. (2016). *Preventing child abuse and neglect: A technical package for policy, norm, and programmatic activities*. National Center for Injury Prevention and Control-Centers for Disease Control and Prevention.
Fraiberg, S. (Ed.). (1980). *Clinical studies in infant mental health*. Basic Books.
Fraiberg, S., Adelson, E., & Shapiro, V. (1975). Ghosts in the nursery: A psychoanalytic approach to the problems of impaired infant-mother relationships. *Journal of the American Academy of Child Psychiatry, 14*(3), 387–421. https://doi.org/10.1016/s0002-7138(09)61442-4
Frattaroli, J. (2006). Experimental disclosure and its moderators: A meta-analysis. *Psychological Bulletin, 132*, 823–865. https://doi.org/10.1037/0033-2909.132.6.823
Freud, A. (1965). *Normality and pathology in childhood: Assessments of development*. IUP.
Freud, S. (1901). *The psychopathology of everyday life* (Standard ed., Vol. 6). The Hogarth Press.
Freud, S. (1915). *The unconscious* (Standard ed., Vol. 14, pp. 159–204). The Hogarth Press.
Freud, S. (1920). *Beyond the pleasure principle* (Standard ed., Vol. 18, pp. 7–64). The Hogarth Press.
Freud, S. (1921). *Group psychology and the analysis of the ego* (Standard ed., Vol. 18, pp. 67–143). The Hogarth Press.

Freud, S. (1926). *Inhibitions, symptoms, and anxiety* (Standard ed., Vol. 20, pp. 87–172). The Hogarth Press.
Freud, S. (1927). *The future of an illusion* (Standard ed., Vol. 21, pp. 5–56). The Hogarth Press.
Freud, S. (1933). *New introductory lectures on psycho-analysis* (Standard ed., Vol. 22). The Hogarth Press.
Galatzer-Levy, R. M. (2017). *Nonlinear psychoanalysis: Notes from forty years of chaos and complexity theory*. Routledge.
Galatzer-Levy, R. M., & Cohler, B. J. (1993). *The essential other: A developmental psychology of the self*. Basic Books.
Gardiner, R. (1983). *Self-inquiry*. Analytic Press, 1989.
Gedo, J. E. (1979). *Beyond interpretation*. International Universities Press.
Gedo, J. E. (2005). *Psychoanalysis as biological science: A comprehensive theory*. The Johns Hopkins University Press.
Geisel, T. S. (1960). *Green eggs and ham, by Dr. Seuss*. Beginner Books (Random House).
Geissman, C., & Geissman, P. (1998). *A history of child psychoanalysis*. Routledge.
George, M. S., Ketter, T. A., Parekh, P., Horowitz, B., Herscovitch, P., & Post, R. M. (1995). Brain activity during transient sadness and happiness in healthy women. *American Journal of Psychiatry, 152*(3), 341–351. https://doi.org/10.1176/ajp.152.3.341
Gershoff, E. T. (2002). Corporal punishment by parents and associated child behaviors and experiences: A meta-analytic and theoretical review. *Psychological Bulletin, 128*(4), 539–579. www.apa.org/pubs/journals/releases/bul-1284539.pdf
Gershoff, E. T. (2008). *Report on physical punishment in the United States: What research tells us about its effects on children*. Center for Effective Discipline.
Gershoff, E. T., & Grogan-Kaylor, A. (2016). Spanking and child outcomes: Old controversies and new meta-analyses. *Journal of Family Psychology, 30*(4), 453–469. https://doi.org/10.1037/fam0000191
Goldberg, A. (2015). *The brain, the mind, and the self: A psychoanalytic road map*. Routledge.
Goleman, D. (1995). *Emotional intelligence*. Bantam Dell Books.
Goodfriend, M. (1993). Treatment of attachment disorder of infancy in a neonatal intensive care unit. *Pediatrics, 91*(1), 139–142.
Gopnik, A. (2010, July). How babies think. *Scientific American*, 76–81.
Gopnik, A., Meltzoff, A. N., & Kuhl, P. K. (1999). *The scientist in the crib: Minds, brains, and how children learn*. William Morrow and Company, Inc.
Gould, S. J. (1993). *Eight little piggies: Reflections in natural history*. W. W. Norton & Company.
Gray, P. (2013). *Free to learn: Why unleashing the instinct to play will make our children happier, more self-reliant, and better students for life*. Basic Books.
Greenberg, J. R., & Mitchell, S. A. (1983). *Object relations in psychoanalytic theory*. Harvard University Press.
Greenson, R. R. (1960). Empathy and its vicissitudes. *International Journal of Psychoanalysis, 41*, 418–424.
Greenspan, S. I. (1992). *Infancy and early childhood: The practice of clinical assessment and intervention with emotional and developmental challenges*. International Universities Press.
Greenspan, S. I. (1997). *Developmentally based psychotherapy*. International Universities Press.
Grinker, R. R. (1956). *Toward a unified theory of human behavior*. Basic Books.
Heilmann, A., Mehey, A., Watt, R. G., Kelly, Y., Durrant, J. E., van Turnhout, J., & Gershoff, E. T. (2021). Physical punishment and child outcomes: A narrative review of prospective studies. *Lancet, 398*(10297). https://doi.org/10.1016/s0140-6736(21)00582-1

Hoffman, L. (2007). Do children get better when we interpret their defenses against painful feelings? *Psychoanalytic Study of the Child*, *62*, 291–313. https://doi.org/10.1080/00797308.2007.11800793

Hoffman, L., & Prout, T. A. (2020). Helping parents spare the rod: Addressing their unbearable emotions. *Psychoanalytic Study of the Child*, *73*, 46–61.

Hoffman, L., Rice, T., & Prout, T. (2016). *Manual of regulation-focused psychotherapy for children (RFP-C) with externalizing behaviors: A psychodynamic approach*. Routledge.

Holden, G. W. (2020). Why do parents hit their children? From cultural to unconscious determinants. *The Psychoanalytic Study of the Child*, *73*, 10–29.

Holden, G. W., Williamson, P. A., & Holland, G. W. O. (2014). Eavesdropping on the family: A pilot investigation of corporal punishment in the home. *Journal of Family Psychology*, *28*(3), 401–406.

Holinger, P. C. (1987). *Violent deaths in the United States: An epidemiologic study of suicide, homicide, and accidents*. Guilford Press.

Holinger, P. C. (1989). A developmental perspective on psychotherapy and psychoanalysis. *American Journal of Psychiatry*, *146*(11), 1404–1412. https://doi.org/10.1176/ajp.146.11.1404

Holinger, P. C. (1999). Noninterpretive interventions in psychoanalysis and psychotherapy: A developmental perspective. *Psychoanalytic Psychology*, *16*(2), 233–253. https://psycnet.apa.org/doi/10.1037/0736-9735.16.2.233

Holinger, P. C. (2003). *What babies say before they can talk: The nine signals infants use to express their feelings*. Simon & Schuster.

Holinger, P. C. (2008). Further issues in the psychology of affect and motivation: A developmental perspective. *Psychoanalytic Psychology*, *25*(3), 425–42. https://doi.org/10.1037/0736-9735.25.3.425

Holinger, P. C. (2016). Further considerations of theory, technique, and affect in child psychoanalysis: Two prelatency cases. *International Journal of Psychoanalysis*, *97*(5), 1279–97. https://doi.org/10.1111/1745-8315.12366

Holinger, P. C. (2020). The problem of physical punishment and its persistence: The potential roles of psychoanalysis. *The Psychoanalytic Study of the Child*, *73*, 1–9. https://doi.org/10.1080/00797308.2020.1690856

Holinger, P. C. (2021). School safety and violence: Enhancing organizational and clinical responses. *International Journal of Applied Psychoanalytic Studies*, *18*(3), 294–299. https://doi.org/10.1002/aps.1725

Holinger, P. C., Offer, D., & Ostrov, E. (1987). Suicide and homicide in the United States: An epidemiologic study of violent deaths, population changes, and potential for prediction. *American Journal of Psychiatry*, *144*(2), 215–219. https://doi.org/10.1176/ajp.144.2.215

Hubbard, J. (2018). *White sheets to brown babies*. Sakshi Press.

Huntington, C. (2014). *Failure to flourish: How law undermines family relationships*. Oxford University Press.

Huntington, C. (2020). The legal framework governing corporal punishment. *Psychoanalytic Study of the Child*, *73*(1), 91–95.

Hurry, A. (1998). *Psychoanalysis and developmental therapy*. International Universities Press.

Izard, C. E. (1971). *The face of emotion*. Appleton-Century-Crofts.

Izard, C. E. (1977). *Human emotions*. Plenum Press.

Jacobs, T. (1991). *The use of the self: Countertransference and communication in the analytic situation*. International University Press.

Kagan, J. (1981). *The second year: The emergence of self-awareness*. Harvard University Press.

Kahneman, D. (2011). *Thinking, fast and slow*. Farrar, Straus and Giroux.

Katan, A. (1961). Some thoughts about the role of verbalization in early childhood. *Psychoanalytic Study of the Child*, *16*, 184–188.
Kelly, D. J., Quinn, P. C., Slater, A. M., Lee, H., Gibson, A., Smith, M., Ge, L., & Pascalis, O. (2005). Three-month-olds, but not newborns, prefer own-race faces. *Developmental Science*, *8*, F31–F36. http://doi.org/10.1111/j.1467-7687.2005.0434a.x
Kelly, V. C., & Lamia, M. C. (2018). *The upside of shame: Therapeutic interventions using the positive aspects of a "negative" emotion*. W. W. Norton & Company.
Kernberg, O. F. (1975). *Borderline conditions and pathological narcissism*. Jason Aronson.
Kernberg, O. F. (1984). *Severe personality disorders: Psychotherapeutic strategies*. Yale University Press.
Kernberg, O. F. (2020). Malignant narcissism and large group regression. *Psychoanalytic Quarterly*, *89*(1), 1–24. https://doi.org/10.1080/00332828.2020.1685342
Kimmel, M. (2013). *Angry white men: American masculinity at the end of an era*. Nation Books.
Kimmel, M. (2018). *Healing from hate: How young men get into—and out of—violent extremism*. University of California Press.
Kircanski, K., Lieberman, M. D., & Craske, M. G. (2012). Feelings into words: Contributions of language to exposure therapy. *Psychological Science*, *23*(10), 1086–1091.
Knapp, P. H. (1987). Some contemporary contributions to the study of emotions. *Journal of the American Psychoanalytic Association*, *35*(1), 205–248. https://doi.org/10.1177/000306518703500112
Kohut, H. (1959). Introspection, empathy and psychoanalysis. *Journal of the American Psychoanalytic Association*, *7*, 459–483. https://doi.org/10.1177/000306515900700304
Kohut, H. (1966). Forms and transformations of narcissism. *Journal of the American Psychoanalytic Association*, *14*(2), 243–272. https://doi.org/10.1177/000306516601400201
Kohut, H. (1971). *The analysis of the self: A systematic approach to the psychoanalytic treatment of narcissistic personality disorders*. International Universities Press.
Kohut, H. (1972). Thoughts on narcissism and narcissistic rage. *The Psychoanalytic Study of the Child*, *27*, 360–400. https://doi.org/10.1080/00797308.1972.11822721
Kohut, H. (1977). *The restoration of the self*. International Universities Press.
Kohut, H. (1984). *How does analysis cure?* University of Chicago Press.
Kohut, H. (1985). *Self psychology and the humanities* (C. B. Strozier, ed.). W. W. Norton & Company.
Kohut, H. (1994). *The curve of life: Correspondence of Heinz Kohut, 1923–1981* (G. Cocks, ed.). The University of Chicago Press.
Kohut, H., & Wolfe, E. S. (1978). The disorders of the self and their treatment. *International Journal of Psycho-Analysis*, *59*, 413–425. www.sakkyndig.com/psykologi/artvit/kohut1978.pdf
Kohut, T. A. (2011). Mirror image of the nation: An investigation of Kaiser Wilhelm II's leadership of the Germans. In C. B. Strozier, D. Offer, & O. Abdyli (Eds.), *The leader: Psychological essays* (2nd ed.). Springer.
Kuhl, P. K. (2015, November). Baby talk. *Scientific American*, 64–69.
Lament, C. M. (n.d.). *The complementary perspectives of linear and non-linear development: Why we need them both in psychoanalytic practice* [Unpublished manuscript].
Lane, R. D., & Nadel, L. (Eds.). (2020). *Neuroscience of enduring change: Implications for psychotherapy*. Oxford University Press.
Lane, R. D., & Schwartz, G. (1987). Levels of emotional awareness: A cognitive developmental theory and its application to psychopathology. *American Journal of Psychiatry*, *144*(2), 133–143.
Langer, S. (1967). *Mind: An essay on human feelings* (Vol. I). The Johns Hopkins Press.
Lansky, M., & Morrison, A. (Eds.). (1997). *The widening scope of shame*. Analytic Press.

Lear, J. (2015). The fundamental rule and fundamental value of psychoanalysis. *Journal of the American Psychoanalytic Association, 63*(3), 511–527. https://doi.org/10.1177/0003065115585808

Lecours, S., & Bouchard, M.-A. (1997). Dimensions of mentalisation: Outlining levels of psychic transformation. *International Journal of Psychoanalysis, 78*(5), 855–875.

Lewin, K. (1943). Problems of research in the social sciences. In *Resolving conflicts and field theory in social science*. American Psychological Association, 1997.

Lewis, M. (2017). *The undoing project: A friendship that changed our minds*. W. W. Norton & Company.

Lieberman, M. D., Eisenberger, N. I., Crockett, M. J., Tom, S. B., Pfeifer, J. H., & Way, B. W. (2007). Putting feelings into words: Affect labeling disrupts amygdala activity in response to affective stimuli. *Psychological Science, 18*(5), 421–428. https://doi.org/10.1111/j.1467-9280.2007.01916.x

Lifton, R. J. (2000). *The Nazi doctors: Medical killing and the psychology of genocide*. Basic Books.

Lifton, R. J. (2020). Owning reality: Reflections on cultism and zealotry. *Journal of the American Psychoanalytic Association, 68*(3), 413–432. https://doi.org/10.1177/0003065120937064

Litowitz, B. E. (2014). Coming to terms with intersubjectivity: Keeping language in mind. *Journal of the American Psychological Association, 62*, 294–312.

Lowder, G., Bucci, W., Maskit, B., & Christian, C. (2007). Poster summaries II. Human development: Intersections with psychoanalytic perspectives: It's hard to say: The challenge of connecting emotions and language for first-time mothers. *Journal of the American Psychoanalytic Association, 55*(1), 265–269.

Mayr, E. (2001). *What evolution is*. Basic Books.

McCullough, D. (2002). *John Adams*. Simon & Schuster Paperbacks.

McCullough, D. (2015). *The Wright brothers*. Simon & Schuster.

Meloy, J. R. (Ed.). (2001). *The mark of Cain: Psychoanalytic insight and the psychopath*. American Psychological Association.

Mercier, H., & Sperber, D. (2017). *The enigma of reason*. Harvard University Press.

Miller, A. (2008). *The drama of the gifted child: The search for the true self* (revised and updated with a new afterward). Basic Books (Originally published as *Das Drama des begabten Kindes*, Suhrkamp Verlag, 1979).

Modell, A. H. (1976). "The holding environment" and the therapeutic action of psychoanalysis. *Journal of the American Psychoanalytic Association, 24*, 285–307.

Morrison, A. P. (1989). *Shame: The underside of narcissism*. Analytic Press.

Nathanson, D. L. (1992). *Shame and pride: Affect, sex, and the birth of the self*. W. W. Norton & Company.

Nathanson, D. L. (Ed.). (1996). *Knowing feeling: Affect, script, and psychotherapy*. W. W. Norton & Company.

Newman, K. (1999). The usable analyst: The role of the affective engagement of the analyst in reaching usability. *The Annual of Psychoanalysis, 26/27*, 175–194.

Novick, J., & Novick, K. K. (2020). Why won't they learn: Unconscious underpinnings of corporal punishment. *The Psychoanalytic Study of the Child, 73*, 62–72.

Novick, K. K., & Novick, J. (2005). *Working with parents makes therapy work*. Jason Aronson.

Offer, D., Offer, M. K., & Ostrov, E. (2004). *Regular guys: 34 years beyond adolescence*. Kluwer Academic/Plenum Publishers.

Österman, K., Björkqvist, K., & Wahlbeck, K. (2014). Twenty-eight years after the complete ban on the physical punishment of children in Finland: Trends and psychosocial concomitants. *Aggressive Behavior, 40*(6), 568–581. https://doi.org/10.1002/ab.21537

Österman, K., Björkqvist, K., & Wahlbeck, K. (2018). A decrease in victimization from physical punishment in Finland in 1934–2014: An evidence of an emerging culture of nonviolent parenting. *Eurasian Journal of Medicine and Oncology, 2*(4), 221–230. www.ejmo.org/10.14744/ejmo.2018.0027/pdf/

Panksepp, J. (1998). *Affective neuroscience: The foundation of human and animal emotions.* Oxford University Press.

Panksepp, J. (Ed.). (2004). *Textbook of biological psychiatry.* Wiley-Liss, Inc.

Panksepp, J., & Biven, L. (2012). *Archaeology of the mind: Neuroevolutionary origins of human emotions.* W. W. Norton & Company.

Paradiso, S., Robinson, R. G., Andreasen, N. C., Downhill, J. E., Davidson, R. J., Kirchner, P. T., Watkins, G. L., Ponto, L. L. B., & Hichwa, R. D. (1997). Emotional activation of limbic circuitry in elderly normal subjects in a PET study. *American Journal of Psychiatry, 154*(3), 384–389. http://doi.org/10.1176/ajp.154.3.384

Pelly, J. (2021, September). Jewel reflects on surviving youth homelessness and influencing Taylor Swift. *United Hemispheres,* 79–84.

Pennebaker, J. W., & Chung, C. K. (2011). Expressive writing: Connections to physical and mental health. In H. S. Friedman (Ed.), *The Oxford handbook of health psychology* (pp. 417–437). Oxford University Press.

Phillips, A. (1988). *Winnicott.* Penguin.

Piaget, J., & Inhelder, B. (1969). *The psychology of the child.* Basic Books (Original work published in French 1966).

Pine, F. (1990). *Drive, ego, object, and self: A synthesis for clinical work.* Basic Books.

Pink, D. H. (2009). *Drive: The surprising truth about what motivates us.* Riverhead Books.

Plutchik, R. (1962). *The emotions: Facts, theory and a new model.* Random House.

Rapaport, D. (1953). On the psychoanalytic theory of affects. *International Journal of Psychoanalysis, 34,* 177–198.

Rapaport, D. (1967). On the psychoanalytic theory of affects. *International Journal of Psychoanalysis.* In M. M. Gill (Ed.), *Collected papers* (pp. 476–512). Basic Books (Original work published 1953).

Reiman, E. M., Lane, R. D., Ahern, G. L., Schwartz, G. E., Davidson, R. J., Friston, K. J., Yun, L. S., & Chen, K. (1997). Neuroanatomical correlates of externally and internally generated human emotion. *American Journal of Psychiatry, 154*(7), 918–925.

Roberts, D. (2002). *Shattered bonds: The color of child welfare.* Basic Books.

Rosenblitt, D. L. (2009). Where do you want the killing done? An exploration of hatred of children. *Annual of Psychoanalysis 36,* 203–215.

Rousseau, J. J. (1782). *The confessions.* Random House, 1945.

Russell, B. (1960). *Bertrand Russell speaks his mind* (1st ed.). World Publishing Co.

Rutherford, A. (2020). *How to argue with a racist: What our genes do (and don't) say about human difference.* The Experiment, LLC.

Salomonsson, B. (2006). The impact of words on children with ADHD and DAMP: Consequences for psychoanalytic technique. *International Journal of Psychoanalysis, 87*(Pt. 4), 1026–1047. https://doi.org/10.1516/eyq4-21hh-1kqj-2wme

Salomonsson, B. (2014). *Psychoanalytic therapy with infants and parents: Practice, theory, and results.* Routledge.

Salomonsson, B. (2016). Infantile defences in parent-infant psychotherapy: The example of gaze avoidance. *International Journal of Psychoanalysis, 97*(1), 65–88. https://doi.org/10.1111/1745-8315.12331

Sander, L. W. (1962). Issues in early mother-child interaction. *Journal of the American Academy of Child Psychiatry, 1,* 141–166.

Saslow, E. (2018). *Rising out of hatred: The awakening of a former white nationalist.* Doubleday.

Schore, A. N. (1994). *Affect regulation and the origin of the self: The neurobiology of emotional development*. Erlbaum.
Sege, R. D., Siegel, B. S., & Council on Child Abuse and Neglect, Committee on Psychosocial Aspects of Child and Family Health. (2018). Effective discipline to raise healthy children. *Pediatrics, 142*(6), e20183112.
Slochower, J. (1996). Holding and the fate of the analyst's subjectivity. *Psychoanalytic Dialogue, 6*(3), 323–353. https://doi.org/10.1080/10481889609539123
Solms, M. (2021). Revision of drive theory. *Journal of the American Psychoanalytic Association, 69*(6), 1033–1091. https://doi.org/10.1177/00030651211057041
Spira, N. (2020). Why can't we see it? *The Psychoanalytic Study of the Child, 73*, 96–108.
Spitz, R. A. (1945). Hospitalism—An inquiry into the genesis of psychiatric conditions in early childhood. *Psychoanalytic Study of the Child, 1*, 53–74.
Spitz, R. A. (1965). *The first year of life: A psychoanalytic study of normal and deviant development of object relations*. International Universities Press.
Spriet, C., Abassi, E., Hochmann, J.-R., & Papeo, L. (2022). Visual object categorization in infancy. *Proceedings of the National Academy of Sciences, 119*(8), e2105866119.
Sroufe, L. A., & Waters, E. (1977). Attachment as an organizational construct. *Child Development, 48*(4), 1184–1199. https://doi.org/10.2307/1128475
Stern, D. N. (1985). *The interpersonal world of the infant: A view from psychoanalysis and developmental psychology*. Basic Books.
Straus, M. A., Douglas, E. M., & Medeiros, R. A. (2014). *The primordial violence: Spanking children, psychological development, violence, and crime*. Routledge.
Strozier, C. B., & Mart, D. (2017). The politics of constructed humiliation: Psychoanalytic perspectives on war, terrorism and genocide. *Research in Psychoanalysis, 1*, 27–36.
Strozier, C. B., Pinteris, K., Kelley, K., & Cher, D. (2022). *The new world of self: Heinz Kohut's transformation of psychoanalysis and psychotherapy*. Oxford University Press.
Strozier, C. B., Terman, D. M., & Jones, J. W. (Eds.). (2010). *The fundamentalist mindset: Psychological perspectives on religion, violence, and history*. Oxford University Press.
Sugarman, A. (2009). Child versus adult psychoanalysis: Two processes or one? *International Journal of Psychoanalysis, 90*(6), 1255–1276. https://doi.org/10.1111/j.1745-8315.2009.00212.x
Taylor, G. J., Bagby, R. M., & Parker, J. D. A. (1997). *Disorders of affect regulation: Alexithymia in medical and psychiatric illness*. Cambridge University Press.
Terman, D. M. (2010a). Theories of group psychology, paranoia, and rage. In C. B. Strozier, D. M. Terman, & J. W. Jones (Eds.), *The fundamentalist mindset: Psychological perspectives on religion, violence, and history* (pp. 47–61). Oxford University Press.
Terman, D. M. (2010b). Fundamentalism and the paranoid gestalt. In C. B. Strozier, D. M. Terman, & J. W. Jones (Eds.), *The fundamentalist mindset: Psychological perspectives on religion, violence, and history* (pp. 16–28). Oxford University Press.
Terman, D. M. (2021). The negative selfobject. *Psychoanalysis, Self and Context, 16*(4), 380–389. https://doi.org/10.1080/24720038.2020.1870981
Thomas, A., & Chess, S. (1977). *Temperament and development*. Brunner/Mazel.
Tolpin, P., & Tolpin, M. (Eds.). (1996). *Heinz Kohut: The Chicago Institute lectures*. The Analytic Press.
Tomkins, S. S. (1962). *Affect imagery consciousness: Vol. I. The positive affects*. Springer.
Tomkins, S. S. (1963). *Affect imagery consciousness: Vol. II. The negative affects*. Springer.
Tomkins, S. S. (1981). The quest for primary motives: Biography and autobiography of an idea. *Journal of Personality and Social Psychology, 41*(2), 306–329. https://doi.org/10.1037/0022-3514.41.2.306
Tomkins, S. S. (1991). *Affect imagery consciousness: Vol. III. The negative affects: Anger and fear*. Springer.

Tomkins, S. S. (1992). *Affect imagery consciousness: Vol. IV. Cognition: Duplication and transformation of information*. Springer.
Torre, J. B., & Lieberman, M. D. (2018). Putting feelings into words: Affect labeling as implicit emotion regulation. *Emotion Review, 10*(2), 116–124. https://doi.org/10.1177/1754073917742706
Tyson, P. (2005). Affects, agency, and self-regulation: Complexity theory in the treatment of children with anxiety and disruptive behavior disorders. *Journal of the American Psychoanalytic Association, 53*(1), 159–187. https://doi.org/10.1177/00030651050530012201
Tyson, P. (2009). Research in child psychoanalysis: Twenty-five-year follow-up of a severely disturbed child. *Journal of the American Psychoanalytic Association, 57*(4), 919–945. https://doi.org/10.1177/0003065109342881
Ullrich, V. (2016). *Hitler: Ascent 1889–1939* (J. Chase, Trans.). Alfred A. Knopf.
Ullrich, V. (2020). *Hitler: Downfall 1939–1945* (J. Chase, Trans.). Knopf Doubleday.
Valeros, J. A. (1989). Coercion—Technical problems in the psychoanalysis of children. *Psychoanalytic Study of the Child, 44*, 165–187.
Vivona, J. M. (2012). Is there a nonverbal period of development? *Journal of the American Psychoanalytic Association, 60*(2), 231–265. https://doi.org/10.1177/0003065112438767
Vivona, J. M. (2014). Introduction: How does talking cure? *Journal of the American Psychoanalytic Association, 62*(6), 1025–1027. https://doi.org/10.1177/0003065114557482
Vivona, J. M. (2019). The interpersonal words of the infant: Implications of current infant language research for psychoanalytic theories of infant development, language, and therapeutic action. *Psychoanalytic Quarterly, 88*(4), 685–725.
von Bertalanffy, L. (1968). *General systems theory: Foundations, development, applications*. George Braziller, Inc.
Weinberg, S. (1977). *The first three minutes: A modern view of the origin of the universe*. Basic Books.
Weiss, S. (1981). Reflections on the psychoanalytical process with special emphasis on child analysis and self analysis. *Annual of Psychoanalysis, IX*, 43–56.
White, R. C., Jr. (2005). *The eloquent president: A portrait of Lincoln through his words*. Random House.
Wilkerson, D. C. (1981). Children's dreams—1900–1980. *Annual of Psychoanalysis, 9*, 57–71.
Winnicott, D. W. (1949). Hate in the counter-transference. *International Journal of Psychoanalysis, 30*, 69–74.
Winnicott, D. W. (1953). Transitional objects and transitional phenomena—A study of the first not-me possession. *International Journal of Psychoanalysis, 34*, 89–97.
Winnicott, D. W. (1958). *Collected papers: Through paediatrics to psycho-analysis*. Tavistock Publications.
Winnicott, D. W. (1960). Ego distortion in terms of true and false self. In *The maturational processes and the facilitating environment* (pp. 140–152). International Universities Press.
Winnicott, D. W. (1963). Training for child psychology. *Journal of Child Psychology and Psychiatry, 4*, 85–91.
Winnicott, D. W. (1965a). *The maturational processes and the facilitating environment*. International Universities Press.
Winnicott, D. W. (1965b). Psychiatric disorder in terms of infantile maturational processes. In *The maturational processes and the facilitating environment* (pp. 230–241). International Universities Press.
Winnicott, D. W. (1971). *Playing and reality*. Routledge.
Yanof, J. (1996). Language, communication, and transference in child analysis. I. Selective mutism: The medium is the message. *Journal of the American Psychoanalytic Association, 44*(1), 79–100. https://doi.org/10.1177/000306519604400105

Yanof, J. (2019). Play in the analytic setting: The development and communication of meaning in child analysis. *International Journal of Psychoanalysis*, *100*(6), 1390–1404. https://doi.org/10.1080/00207578.2019.1642758

Young-Bruehl, E. (2012). *Childism: Confronting prejudice against children*. Yale University Press.

Index

Please note that *italicized* page numbers in this index indicate figures, and page numbers in **bold** indicate tables.

Adams, John 57, 72
Adler, G. 60
Affect Imagery Consciousness, Volume III (Tomkins) 14
affects: affective responses, examples of 26; amplification of 24–25; bias and prejudice in individuals 139; bias and prejudice on group level 141–143; clinical implications 27–31; current concepts of 19–20, 32–33; early development and sense of self 54–62; early verbalization of 95–97; function of 20–26; labeling of 85–86; as "messy system" 5–6; as motivator of behavior 6–8, 24–25; negative 48; nine primary affects 14–17, **15**, *16*; overview and evolution of the concept 4–5, 10–14; and physical punishment 121–123, 125, 129, 131; playing and creating 46–53; positive vs. negative 19–20; and self in clinical settings 60–62; transformations of 31; translation into words 84–85, 87–94
Aichhorn, August 6
Ainsworth, M. 33
alexithymia 102
American Academy of Child and Adolescent Psychiatry (AACAP) 128
American Academy of Pediatrics (AAP) 128
American Medical Association (AMA) 128
American Psychiatric Association (APA) 128
American Psychoanalytic Association 128

American Psychological Association (APA) 128
anger 63–71; clinical and theoretical issues 65–67; and fear 64–65
Aristotle 63
attachment theory 33, 56

Basch, Michael Franz 8, 11, 70–71, *98*; on affects, development and role 14, 17; defense against affect 31; on empathy 98, 99; feelings vs. emotions, 17–18
Bateson, Gregory 13
behavior: behavioral change 31, 110, 124; focus on 126–127, 130; motivators of 6–8, 24–25
Beiser, Helen 34
bias, prejudice and violence 133–146; definitions 134; in groups and society 141–144; in individuals 138–141; prejudice, development of 144–146
Birdwhistell, Ray 13
Black, Derek 141, 142, 145–146
Black Like Me (Griffin) 141
Blumenthal, Sidney xvi
Bonamici, Suzanne 128, 132
Bouchard, M.-A. 102
Bowlby, J. 33
Brinich, P. 102
Buie, D. 60

Centers for Disease Control and Prevention (CDC) 128
Chanute, Octave 93–94

child development: advances and changing approaches 8–9; affects and early interactions 55–57; affects translated into words 84–85, 87–94; definitions 9; dreams 66–67; earliest feelings 4, 55, 85, 87, 95, 96–97, 98; early cognition 74, 75–77, 79–80; interest, affect of 39–42; language 81–86; linear models 8; nonlinear models 8–9; significance of 3–4; *see also* infant development

child therapy: parents' role 56; and play 51–53

Clay, Lucius D. 145

cognition: bias and prejudice in individuals 140; bias and prejudice on group level 143–144; complex, and human relationships 74–75; dysfunction and disorders 78–79; early 74, 75–77, 79–80; learning and education 78; as "messy system" 5–6; as motivator of behavior 6–8; overview and definitions 4–5, 72–74; and physical punishment 123, 126, 129, 131; and relationships 74–75

competence theory 8

conspiracy beliefs xv, 141

contagion of emotion 64, 122–123

corporal punishment 116–132; and affects 121–123, 125, 129, 131; and cognition 123, 126, 129, 131; contributing factors 118–119; definitions 118; impact of 119–120; international trends 126–128; and language 123–124, 126, 129, 131; prevention of 129–132; societal level 125–126

creating, playing, and affects xiv, 46–53

cults 134–137, 142

cultural relativism 13

Curie, Marie 31

curiosity 34–36, 42–43; and fear 31; interference with 43–45; and prevention of physical punishment 129; and self-reflection 62; *see also* interest, affect of

Damasio, A. R. 37

Darwin, Charles *12*; cognition and bias in individuals 140; *Descent of Man, The* 11–12, 36; evolutionary paleontology 57; *Expression of the Emotions in Man and Animals, The* 12, 35–36, 42; *Origin of Species* 11, 148; playful nature 47–48

decontamination scripts 33, 141

Demos, Virginia 8; on affects, development and role 14; attachment theory 33; on curiosity, impairment of 44; on early interactions 56

Descent of Man, The (Darwin) 11–12, 36

development *see* child development; human development; infant development

differential emotions theory 14

disgust 23–24; decontamination scripts 141

dissmell 14, 23–24

Doner, Kalia 146

Douglas, Emily 119

Douglass, Frederick 141

Drama of the Gifted Child, The (Miller) 50

dreams 66–67

Drive, Ego, Object & Self (Pine) 60

Duchenne, G. B. 11

Durrant, Joan 119, 127, *127*

Dylan, Bob 59

earliest feelings 4, 55, 85, 87, 95, 96–97, 98; *see also* affects; child development; emotion

Einstein, Albert 34

Ekman, Paul 12, *14*; emotion, expression of 13

Emancipation Proclamation 149

emotion: contrasted with feelings 17–18, 98; Darwin on 35, 42; and early development 4, 55, 85, 87, 95, 96–97, 98; emotional regulation 85–86; expression of 12–14, 95, 96–97; neurobiology of 37; and trauma 20

Emotional Intelligence (Goleman) 73

empathic understanding 18

empathy 97–100

enjoyment and interest 38–39

Ensom, R. 119

evolution 11–12, 57, 143–144, 148–149

Expression of the Emotions in Man and Animals, The (Darwin) 12, 35–36, 42

facial expressions 11, 14–17, **15,** *16*; facial muscles *17*; facial-signaling system 39

Fajardo, Barbara 87

fear 123; and anger 64–65; and interest 37; *see also* rage

feelings 17–18; feelings vs. emotions 17–18, 98; learning words for 91; *see also* emotions

Ferro, A. 102

First Three Minutes, The (Weinberg) 57–58
"floortime" 40–41, 50
Floyd, George 141
Fonagy, P. 33
Fraiberg, Selma 44
Freud, Anna *52*; on play 51
Freud, Sigmund *13*; on affect 12–13; cognition and bias in individuals 140; on cognitive processes 72; defense against affect 31; individual vs. group work 114; major discoveries of 12; playing and creating 50–51
Fundamentalist Mindset, The (Strozier et al.) 114–115
Future of an Illusion, The 58

Gardiner, R. 35
Gedo, John 11, 20, 66, *69*; on affective reactions 14, 26, 70; on disorders of cognition 79; language and encoding of affect 102; on self-understanding 31
Gershoff, Elizabeth *117*, 119
Gettysburg Address (Lincoln) 143
"Ghosts in the Nursery" (Fraiberg) 44
Gilmore, K. 102
Global Pathways to Abolishing Physical Punishment (Durrant & Smith) 127
Goldberg, Arnold 54
Goleman, Daniel 73
Gopnik, Alison 42, *76*, 76–77, 80; cognitive studies of infants 100
Gould, Stephen Jay 57, *57*
Green Eggs and Ham (Seuss) 42
Greenson, Ralph 99
Greenspan, Stanley 40–41, *41*, 48, 50; "floortime" 50, 56–57
Griffin, John Howard 141
Grogan-Kaylor, A. 119
group vs. individual psychology 114–115

"Hate in the Counter-Transference" (Winnicott) 122
Heilmann, A. 119
Hitler, Adolf 135–136, 142
Holden, George 118–119, 120, *121*
Holinger, P. C. 14
Holub, Miroslav xiv
hospitalism 55
"House Divided" speech (Lincoln) 3
How to Argue with a Racist (Rutherford) 144

Hubbard, Jvonne 141, 142, 145–146, *146*
Hug-Hellmuth, Hermine 51
human development 3–4; definitions 9; theories of 8–9; *see also* child development
Huntington, Clare 128

"I Have a Dream" speech (King) 143
infant development: infant observation 39–40; innate responses 74; significance of 3–4; *see also* child development
information processing systems: "messy systems" 5–6; as motivators of behavior 6–8; overview 4–5; *see also* affects; cognition; language
initiative, independent center of 40
innate capacities 137–138
inner speech (Vygotsky) 98
interest, affect of 34–45; children and interest 39–40; children's interests, validation of 40–42; and enjoyment 38–39; interference with 43–45; *see also* curiosity
intergenerational violence 142
Interpersonal World of the Infant, The (Stern) 3, 6–7, 50, 74
intragenerational violence 142
Izard, Carroll 14, 37

Jewel (singer) 59

Katan, Anny 66, 85, *88*, 88–89, 96, 102, 123–124, 129
Kernberg, O. F. 139
King, Martin Luther, Jr. 143
Klein, Melanie 51, *51*
Knapp, Peter 11, 70–71; on affects, development and role 17
Kohut, Heinz 48, 54, 58, *60*; affect in clinical process 61; on childhood development 3; on disorders of self 59; empathy 97–98, 99; narcissistic issues, origins of 60; on narcissistic rage 65
Kuhl, Patricia 76, *83*, 83–84

lachrymal glands 41–42
Lament, Claudia 38, 122
Lane, Richard D. *26*; affective processes 26; affects, integration of 17; neurobiology of emotions 37
Langer, Susanne 26
language 81–86; affects translated into words 84–94; assets and liabilities

82; bias and prejudice in individuals 140–141; bias and prejudice on group level 144; development beyond childhood 92–93; early verbalization of affects 95–97; infant capacities 83–84; as "messy system" 5–6; as motivator of behavior 6–8; overview and definitions 4–5, 81–82; parents and children's emotions 84; and physical punishment 123–124, 126, 129, 131; words as weapons 140
learning processes 137–138; and curiosity 43–45
Lecours, S. 102
LeDoux, Joseph 37
Lifton, Robert Jay *134*, 134–135, 141
Lincoln, Abraham xvi, 3, 143, 149
Litowitz, Bonnie 5–6, 87, *92*, 92–93
Lowder, Greg 86

MacArthur, Douglas 145
Maturational Processes and the Facilitating Environment, The (Winnicott) 40
Mayr, Ernst 57
Mead, Margaret 13
Medeiros, Roseanne 119
Meltzoff, Andrew 76
Meregnani, A. 102
Miller, Alice 50
motivators of behavior 6–8, 24–25
Murphy, Chris 128, 132
mutism, selective 43, 101–102

narcissism: narcissistic issues 60, 99, 141, 144; narcissistic rage 65; narcissistic vulnerabilities 59
Narrative of the Life of Frederick Douglass (Douglass) 141
Nathanson, D. L. 14
Nazi Doctors, The (Lifton) 141
negative affects 19–20
neural firing 21–22, *22, 23, 24*
neurobiology of emotions 37
Nicomachean Ethics, The (Aristotle) 63
Night (Wiesel) 141
nuclear self 40

Offer, Dan 78–79
Oman, Jennifer Lock 24, 48
On the Origin of Species (Darwin) 11, 148
Österman, Karin 127

Panksepp, Jaak *38*; on affects, development and role 14; neurobiology of emotions 37
paranoid gestalt 141
parents and children 66; language and children's emotions 84; parents' role in therapy 56; *see also* physical punishment
personality development 58–59
pets as transitional objects 48
Phillips, Adam 56
physical punishment *see* corporal punishment
physiologic drives 17
Piaget, Jean *73*, 73–74
Pine, Fred 60
playing, creating, and affects xiv, 46–53
Playing and Reality (Winnicott) 46
prejudice: case studies 145–146; development of 144–145
Primordial Violence, The (Straus et al.) 119–120
Protecting Our Students in Schools Act 128, 132
Psychoanalysis as Biological Science (Gedo) 20
punishment, physical *see* corporal punishment

racism 144–145; *see also* prejudice
rage 63–64, 68, 69–70; and cults 135; expression of **15**; narcissistic 65; *see also* anger
Rapaport, David 10
Representations of Interactions, Generalized (RIGs) 37
Rising Out of Hatred (Black) 141, 145
Roosevelt, Franklin D. 143
Russell, Bertrand 73
Rutherford, Adam 144

sadness 17, 32
Salomonsson, B. 90
Schore, A. N. 37
Schwartz, G. 17
Scientist in the Crib, The (Gopnik et al.) 42, 76
script theory (Tomkins) 33, 37
SEEKING system (Panksepp) 37
Sege, Robert 128
selective mutism 43, 101–102
self: nuclear self 40; True vs. False 49–50

self-awareness 49–50
self-disorders 60
self-esteem 70–71
self-fragility 60
Self-Made Man, A (Blumenthal) xvi
self-understanding 31
Seuss, Dr. 42
shame 22–23, 70–71; vignette of varied reactions 29–31
Shirer, William 136
Smith, Anne 127
Social Emotional Learning (SEL) 131
social referencing 78
spanking 118; *see also* physical punishment
Speers, Albert 136
Spitz, René 55–56, *55*, 74
Sroufe, L. A. 33
Stern, Daniel 3, *7*; on affects, development and role 14, 17; on children's interests, validation of 40; early childhood development 50; on early interactions 56; infant abilities and cognition 75; *Interpersonal World of the Infant, The* 6–7, 74; on language acquisition 5, 82; model of development 105; Representations of Interactions, Generalized (RIGs) 37
stimulation levels, increase/decrease 21–22
stimulus-response systems 37, 123, 138
Stowe, Harriet Beecher 141
Straus, Murray A. 119, *120*, 128
stress 63–64
Strozier, Chuck *114*
surprise 37

Terman, David 54, 58, 114–115, *114*, 141
Tolpin, Marian 61
Tolpin, Paul 61
Tomkins, Silvan S. 11, *21*; affect model 19, 24–25; affects, development and role 14, 20–21; affects, dictionary of 18; affects, integration of 17; affects in clinical work 28; anger, power of 124; on cognition 72–73, 149; emotion, expression of 12; fear vs. distress 139; General Images 31; on interest, affect of 35–37; negative affects 63; physical punishment 116; playing and creating 47; script theory 33, 37; on stimulus response 138
transitional objects 48–49, 58
trauma 20, 40
Tyson, Phyllis 66, 105–107, *106*

Ullrich, Volker 135–136, 141, 142
Uncle Tom's Cabin (Stowe) 141
United Nations Convention on the Rights of the Child (CRC) 126
Uvalde, Texas, shooting incident 6

Valeros, Jose 53
validation, external 59
verbalization: of affects 89, 95–97; of anger 65–66; feelings/actions/interpersonal skills 109–110
violence 141–142; groups that embrace 133
Volkan, Vamik 133
Vygotsky, Lev 98

Waters, E. 33
Wayward Youth (Aichhorn) 6
Weinberg, Steven 57–58
What Babies Say Before They Can Talk (Holinger) xiii, xvi
White Sheets to Brown Babies (Hubbard) 141, 145–146, *146*
Wiesel, Elie 141
Wilkerson, Cliff *66*, 66–67
Winnicott, Donald 40, *49*; affects translated into words 90; "Hate in the Counter-Transference" 122; narcissistic issues, origins of 60; playing and creating 53; *Playing and Reality* 46; self-awareness 49–50; transitional objects 48–49, 58
Wolfe, E. S. 61
Wright, Wilbur 93–94

Yanof, Judy 66, *101*, 101–102
Young-Bruehl, Elisabeth 133

Milton Keynes UK
Ingram Content Group UK Ltd.
UKHW021319150924
448327UK00014B/182